30/4

How to Use This Book

Look for these special features in this book:

SIDEBARS, **CHARTS**, **GRAPHS**, and original **MAPS** expand your understanding of what's being discussed—and also make useful sources for classroom reports.

FAQs answer common **F**requently **A**sked **Q**uestions about people, places, and things.

WOW FACTORS offer "Who knew?" facts to keep you thinking.

TRAVEL GUIDE gives you tips on exploring the state—either in person or right from your chair!

PROJECT ROOM provides fun ideas for school assignments and incredible research projects. Plus, there's a guide to primary sources—what they are and how to cite them.

Please note: All statistics are as up-to-date as possible at the time of publication.

Consultants: Thomas R. Holtz Jr., Department of Geology, University of Maryland; William Loren Katz; Edward Papenfuse, Maryland State Archivist and Commissioner of Land Patents

Book production by The Design Lab

Library of Congress Cataloging-in-Publication Data
Blashfield, Jean F.
 Maryland / by Jean F. Blashfield.
   p. cm.—(America the beautiful. Third series)
 Includes bibliographical references and index.
 ISBN-13: 978-0-531-18576-6
 ISBN-10: 0-531-18576-1
 1. Maryland—Juvenile literature. I. Title. II. Series.
 F181.3.B58 2008
 975.2—dc22   2007012699

1 2 3 4 5 6 7 8 9 10 R 17 16 15 14 13 12 11 10 09 08

AMERICA ★ THE ★ BEAUTIFUL

Maryland

BY JEAN F. BLASHFIELD

Third Series

Children's Press®
An Imprint of Scholastic Inc.
New York ★ Toronto ★ London ★ Auckland ★ Sydney
Mexico City ★ New Delhi ★ Hong Kong
Danbury, Connecticut

CONTENTS

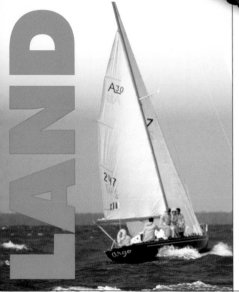

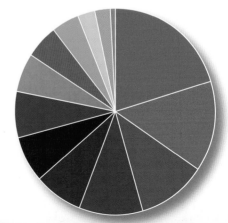

4 GROWTH AND CHANGE

Marylanders play an important role in the struggle to create, build, and protect a new nation. . . . .

MORE MODERN TIMES

5 While Baltimore continued to prosper, other parts of Maryland became suburbs of the nation's capital. . . . .

9 TRAVEL GUIDE

Buzzing cities, colonial history, wild ponies on the beach, Thoroughbreds at the track, the Appalachian Trail, sailing—and so much more. . . . . . .

PROJECT ROOM

★

★

PENNSYLVANIA

Muddy
Creek
Falls

South Mountain
Blue Ridge

Camp David

Fort McHenry

Susquehanna

CUMBERLAND ○

Potomac

Fort Meade

Orioles Park at
Camden Yards

The U.S. Naval
Academy

WEST
VIRGINIA

FREDERICK ○

M A R Y L A N D

BALTIMORE ○

Delaware
Bay

NEW
JERS

ROCKVILLE ○

U.S. Weather
Bureau

★
ANNAPOLIS

Chesapeake Bay
Bridge

DELAWARE

DISTRICT OF
COLUMBIA

Banneker-
Douglass
Museum

SALISBURY ○

Assateague Is
National Seash

Potomac
River

N
W ✦ E
S

Patuxent

Potomac

Chesapeake Bay

Chincoteague
Bay

0   30

Miles

VIRGINIA

Chesapeake Bay

ATLANTIC
OCEAN

QUICK FACTS

State capital: Annapolis
Largest city: Baltimore
Total area: 12,407 square miles
(32,134 sq km)
Highest point: Hoye Crest on
Backbone Mountain, 3,360
feet (1,024 m)
Lowest point: Sea level at the
Atlantic Ocean

Welcome to Maryland!

HOW DID MARYLAND GET ITS NAME?

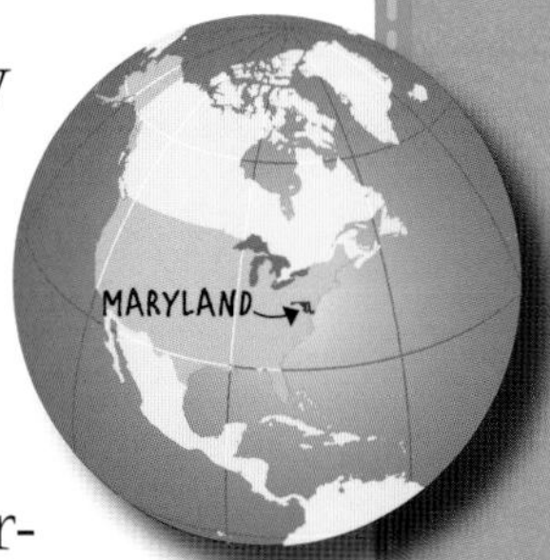

The British king, Charles I, made many people in his Protestant nation angry when he married Henrietta Maria, a French princess of the Catholic faith. Charles needed to marry a Catholic for international political reasons and had hoped to marry a daughter of Philip III of Spain. None of the Spanish princesses was available, so he chose Henrietta Maria instead. In 1635, Charles kept his father's promise to George Calvert, the first Lord Baltimore, to grant Calvert's family a charter for a new colony in America. His son, Cecil Calvert, the second Lord Baltimore, named the new colony *Terra Mariae*, Latin for "Maria's land," in honor of the king's wife. The colony became known as Maryland.

MARYLAND

ATLANTIC OCEAN

8

READ ABOUT

The Potomac River runs among West Virginia, Virginia, and Maryland.

CHAPTER ONE

LAND

★

MARYLAND RANKS 42ND AMONG THE STATES IN GEOGRAPHIC SIZE, WITH A TOTAL AREA OF 12,407 SQUARE MILES (32,134 SQUARE KILOMETERS). In one place, the state is less than 2 miles (3.2 km) from north to south—the narrowest piece of land between two borders anywhere in the United States!—because of the meandering of the Potomac River. But don't let its size fool you. From the 3,360-foot (1,024 meter) Hoye Crest on Backbone Mountain to the Atlantic coastline, Maryland has lots of interesting places to explore.

BORDERS

When you look at a map of Maryland, the most obvious thing you see is that it's split up the middle by a huge arm of the Atlantic Ocean. This is Chesapeake Bay. The shores of the bay do not form any of Maryland's borders. The Potomac River forms the border on the southwest and west with Virginia and West Virginia. The perfectly straight border on the north separates Maryland from Pennsylvania. It is called the Mason-Dixon Line, after the two surveyors who drew the line to settle an argument between the colonies.

A square north-south and east-west border gives Delaware a chunk of the peninsula on the eastern side of Chesapeake Bay. Another mostly straight east-west border on the southern part of the peninsula separates Maryland from Virginia, at least on land. While crossing the bay, the border meanders around some islands, including Smith Island, one of the oldest sites settled by Europeans in Maryland. Only a small portion of the ocean shore belongs to Maryland.

Sailboats race across Chesapeake Bay in the Hammond Regatta.

CHESAPEAKE BAY

A satellite view of Chesapeake Bay

The peninsula on the east side of Chesapeake Bay belongs to three states—Delaware, Maryland, and Virginia. It is often called Delmarva, from the three state names. Most of Delmarva belongs to Maryland. The area is usually referred to as the Eastern Shore.

A square-sided chunk of land is missing from west-central Maryland on the map. That chunk is the District of Columbia. Maryland gave that land to the United States government in 1791. It was supposed to be part of a square

Maryland Topography

Use the color-coded elevation chart to see on the map Maryland's high points (dark red to orange) and low points (green to dark green). Elevation is measured as the distance above or below sea level.

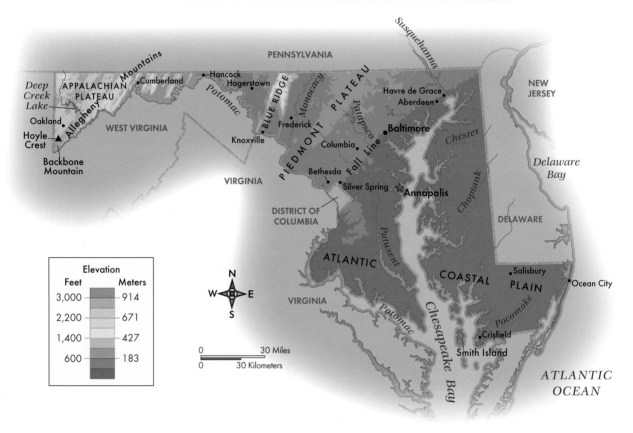

area crossing the Potomac River, part from Maryland and part from Virginia. Virginia's section of the square was returned in 1847, and now all of the District of Columbia is located on land that was originally part of Maryland.

LAND REGIONS

Maryland is divided into three main geographic regions: the Atlantic Coastal Plain along the ocean and Chesapeake Bay, the Piedmont Plateau, and the mountainous west.

The Atlantic Coastal Plain

The Eastern Shore (and part of the Western Shore) is part of the Atlantic Coastal Plain. Also called the **Tidewater**, it is basically flatland that formed from the accumulation of debris shed into the ocean from the mountains farther west millions of years ago. The plain is a fertile area of many rivers and marshes. The land is good for agriculture.

The Coastal Plain ends abruptly in a ridge of hard rock called the Fall Line. This is the edge of the bedrock that forms the hard core of the continent. Rivers often descend the Fall Line as waterfalls. One of the most spectacular sights in Maryland is the Great Falls of the Potomac River. The river crashes down a long series of rocks carved from the hard rock of the Fall Line.

Boats cannot travel from the ocean to west of the Fall Line. Consequently, many of America's first cities were built along the Fall Line. Baltimore was built along the Fall Line of the Patapsco River.

The Great Falls of the Potomac River

WORD TO KNOW

tidewater *low coastal land that is affected by tides*

Piedmont Plateau

West of the Fall Line, the land rises as the Piedmont Plateau. *Piedmont* means "foot of the mountains." It is a land of hills that gradually rise from about 200 feet (61 m) above sea level to about 800 feet (244 m). The Piedmont is also good for agriculture. It has many farms where horses are bred. Maryland's forests begin in the Piedmont.

The Mountainous West

The far western region is the part of Maryland that looks like a triangle on the map. The triangle is formed by the Potomac River and the southern border of Pennsylvania. The mountains here include two ranges that make up part of the huge Appalachian Mountain complex. The easternmost range is the Blue Ridge Mountains. They got their name because, from a distance, they look blue in color. Part of the Blue Ridge is South Mountain, which sounds as if it should be a single mountain, but it is actually a 70-mile- (113 km) long ridge that runs from Knoxville, Maryland, into Pennsylvania. Maryland's part of the Appalachian National Scenic Trail runs along the crest of South Mountain. Frederick and Hagerstown are cities of the Blue Ridge.

At the far western edge of Maryland, in Garrett

Maryland Geo-Facts

Along with the state's geographical highlights, this chart ranks Maryland's land, water, and total area compared to all other states.

Total area; rank	12,407 square miles (32,134 sq km); 42nd
Land; rank	9,774 square miles (25,315 sq km); 42nd
Water; rank	2,633 square miles (6,819 sq km); 18th
Inland water; rank	680 square miles (1,761 sq km); 32nd
Coastal water; rank	1,843 square miles (4,773 sq km); 4th
Territorial water; rank	110 square miles (285 sq km); 20th
Geographic center	Prince Georges, 4.5 miles (7.2 km) northwest of Davidsonville
Latitude	37° 53' N to 39° 43' N
Longitude	75° 4' W to 79° 33' W
Highest point	Hoye Crest on Backbone Mountain, 3,360 feet (1,024 m)
Lowest point	Sea level at the Atlantic Ocean
Largest city	Baltimore
Longest river	Potomac River, 383 miles (665 km), originating in West Virginia

Source: U.S. Census Bureau

Maryland is a small state. It would fit inside California more than 13 times.

Blue Ridge Summit Overlook

County, are the Allegheny Mountains. Located among them is Backbone Mountain, a 10-mile (16 km) ridge. At 3,360 feet (1,024 m), Hoye Crest on Backbone Mountain is the state's highest point. Potomac State Forest surrounds the mountain. The state's largest lake, Deep Creek Lake, and its highest waterfall, Muddy Creek Falls, are also in Garrett County.

Between the Alleghenies and the Blue Ridge is a wide land of ridges and valleys. The city of Cumberland lies in this section, as does Hancock, the town at Maryland's narrowest place.

People and places in Maryland are usually described as being from the Eastern Shore, Southern and Central Maryland, or Western Maryland. Southern and Central Maryland together are often referred to as the Western Shore.

Marsh at the edge of Chesapeake Bay

The basin in which Chesapeake Bay lies may have been formed by a meteorite striking Earth 35 million years ago.

CHESAPEAKE BAY

A European mapmaker named Mercator published a map in 1587 showing, for the first time, the entrance to Chesapeake Bay. Three years later, the name Chesepiooc appeared on a map. Probably the name of an Indian village, it became Chesapeake.

The bay is a product of the last ice age, which ended more than 12,000 years ago. Long before the ice came, a river, the ancient version of the Susquehanna, had created a deep valley through the low-lying land. When the great ice sheet that covered northern North America melted, its waters flowed into the ocean. The rising ocean water filled the river's valley, creating Chesapeake Bay.

The bay we know today is nearly 200 miles (322 km) long from north to south. It varies in width from 3.4 miles (5.5 km) at Aberdeen to about 35 miles (56 km) at the mouth of the Potomac River. The bay is quite shallow, averaging less than 30 feet (9 m). The deepest part is the path the ancient Susquehanna River took before the bay was formed.

Forty-eight major rivers and 100 small tributaries feed into Chesapeake Bay. Together, they drain an area of 64,000 square miles (165,760 sq km).

Chesapeake Bay is one of the great **estuaries** of the world. At the north end of the bay, the water is mostly freshwater, provided by rivers. At the southern end, the water is mostly salt water, brought in from the ocean by tides. This combination provides habitats for both marine and freshwater plants and animals.

The bay is tidal, meaning that the water level in the bay rises and falls at least 1 to 2 feet (0.3 m to 0.6 m) each day. Salt water is heavier than freshwater, so when the tide comes in from the ocean, the salt water sinks and flows northward along the bottom of the bay. That creates one kind of environment. The lighter freshwater on the top creates another kind of environment.

RIVERS ABOUND

There are at least 75 rivers in Maryland. That number is unusually high for such a small state. Also unusual, Maryland doesn't have any natural lakes. All of the bodies of water called lakes—even the biggest, Deep Creek Lake—were made when Marylanders built dams to make reservoirs for storing water.

Five of the eight largest rivers flowing into Chesapeake Bay belong to Maryland, though the Potomac is shared with Virginia and West Virginia.

WORD TO KNOW

estuaries *mouths of rivers where the river's freshwater mixes with the saltwater of the ocean, creating a variety of habitats*

CHESAPEAKE BAY RETRIEVER—THE STATE DOG

In 1807, a ship trading between England and Newfoundland was wrecked off the coast of Maryland. An American ship, the *Canton*, rescuing the crew and cargo, found two Newfoundland puppies. Two Marylanders who helped with the rescue were given the dogs. The dogs were exceptionally good at retrieving ducks for hunters, even in the wintry waters of the bay. The pair, a male and a female of different colors, parented many pups. By 1890, their descendants had settled into a single color, dark brown with a reddish tinge. The American Kennel Club recognizes the Chesapeake Bay retriever as a separate breed.

The Potomac is Maryland's longest river, at 285 miles (459 km). The longest river entirely within Maryland is the Patuxent. It rises in the Piedmont and flows 115 miles (185 km) into Chesapeake Bay. Almost half of its length is estuary. The Choptank is the largest river on the Eastern Shore.

The Susquehanna River in the north is the longest river on the East Coast, but only about 30 miles (48 km) of it are located in Maryland. It flows into Chesapeake Bay at Havre de Grace, carrying about half the freshwater that enters the bay. It also carries more than a quarter of the pollution that reaches the bay, primarily from Pennsylvania.

Many little rivers and creeks contribute to the marshiness of the Eastern Shore. The grasses that grow in these marshes provide important habitat for wildlife of many different kinds.

NATIONAL PARKS

Maryland has a variety of national parklands. They include a canal, several highways, a presidential retreat, two Civil War battlefields, a national seashore, homes of famous people, mountain trails, and even a carousel.

The Catoctin Mountains are part of the Blue Ridge, starting near Emmitsburg. President Franklin D. Roosevelt had a presidential retreat, now called Camp David, built within easy reach of Washington, D.C. Surrounding Camp David is Catoctin Mountain Park.

Assateague Island on the Atlantic coast is a barrier island—a long, narrow accumulation of rocks and sand that protects the mainland behind it from storms. It is 37 miles (60 km) long, running from Ocean City to Chincoteague National Wildlife Refuge in Virginia.

SEE IT HERE!

WILD PONIES OF ASSATEAGUE ISLAND

Wild horses roam free on Assateague Island. They are smaller than regular horses and are usually brown and white. These feral, or wild, horses are thought to be descendants of domestic horses that were brought to the barrier islands in the late 1800s by owners who were trying to avoid paying taxes on their livestock.

Maryland National Park Areas

This map shows some of Maryland's national parks, monuments, preserves, and other areas protected by the National Park Service.

ANIMAL LIFE

Maryland has four national wildlife refuges that are open to the public. Blackwater National Wildlife Refuge is a maze of marshlands on the Eastern Shore. Four rivers wander through it, making it inviting to almost 300 species of birds. It has more nesting bald eagles than anyplace in the eastern United States except Florida. It also has the Delmarva fox squirrel, which is endangered because of loss of woodland habitat.

Also on the Eastern Shore is Eastern Neck National Wildlife Refuge (NWR), located where the Chester River

ENDANGERED ANIMALS

Some animal habitats—both on land and in Maryland's waters—have been changed by growing human populations. Some animal species are in danger of dying out completely. These include several species of whales and sea turtles, as well as the big cat called the puma or cougar. Probably the most famous endangered species on the Eastern Shore is the Delmarva fox squirrel. Larger and heavier than the common gray squirrel, it needs mature forests to thrive. But most of the forests on the Eastern Shore were converted to farmland long ago. Maryland's wildlife refuges are important to preserving these squirrels.

flows into the bay. An important species here is the tundra swan, also called the whistling swan. These are magnificent birds that migrate along the Eastern Shore. But you are more likely to see an invader, the mute swan. Mute swans, which have an orange beak instead of black, are not native to Maryland. Maryland's large population of mute swans stems from only five birds that escaped from captivity in 1962. Zoologists fear that their numbers could soon reach 20,000. Ecologists want to get rid of them because they push out the native tundra swans and they destroy grasses that are an important habitat for other animals.

Martin NWR makes up the northern half of Smith Island in the mouth of the bay. It is home to ospreys, or fish hawks, that live in the island's maze of tidal creeks. The Patuxent Research Refuge in the central Western Shore is unusual

Delmarva fox squirrel

because it is the only NWR created as a center for research on protecting wildlife. Founded in 1936, it occupies one of the largest forested areas in the mid-Atlantic.

Marine Life

Chesapeake Bay is most famous for two animals that have served as food for thousands of years—crabs and oysters. The famous Maryland crab is the blue crab. Its shells are bluish rather than red.

Oysters have been an important food for Marylanders since ancient times, when Native Americans discovered these shelled **invertebrates** living in the waters of Chesapeake Bay. Oysters are also important to the ecology of the bay because their shells build up into **reefs** that support other wildlife. Also, water filters through oysters and is cleaned in the process. Scientists have estimated that in the past, the filtering effect of these animals could clean the entire bay's water in four days!

The diamondback terrapin is Maryland's state reptile. Terrapins are turtles that can thrive in the slightly salty water of the bay. Though these animals used to be a prized food, their numbers have declined. It is illegal to take diamondback terrapins during egg-laying season, which is from the beginning of May to the end of July.

The state fish is the striped bass, sometimes called the rockfish. They spawn (lay eggs) in the rivers of the lower bay. After three to five years in the bay, the striped bass swim into the Atlantic, where they can live for up to 30 years. As with many bay animals, their numbers are declining as the bay becomes overused. In the 1980s, the state put a temporary stop to fishing for striped bass.

WORDS TO KNOW

invertebrates *animals without a backbone*

reefs *ridges of rock or shell that rise near the top of the water, making habitats for other animals*

The diamondback terrapin is the mascot of the University of Maryland.

A great white heron in flight in Assateague National Wildlife Refuge

In the Air and on Land

Because there's so much water in Maryland, most of the state's birds are waterfowl. Gulls, herons, and sandpipers of many species are found along the shores. The Western Shore also has many songbirds and other birds that are common to the continent. Robins, sparrows, vultures, hawks, owls, flycatchers, crows, and others are found throughout its forested areas and suburbs.

Big mammals such as wolves, elk, and cougars once roamed the region, but such spectacular animals are gone from Maryland now. There are still some black bears in the mountainous west. White-tailed deer are plentiful. The remaining mammals are smaller, such as mice, shrews, woodchucks, gray squirrels, opossums, beavers, rabbits, bats, foxes, and muskrats.

PLANT LIFE

With its diverse landscape, Maryland has more variety of plants than most other states. They grow in sandy soil, in boggy wetlands, on rising open plains, or at the foot of mountains. State officials encourage gardeners to grow the kinds of plants that are native to their specific area.

Six plants in Maryland are on the federal endangered species list, owing to the loss of their marshy wetland or coastal plain habitat. They include the swamp pink, Canby's dropwort, and northeastern bulrush.

About 40 percent of Maryland land is still forested. The hardwood forests are mainly of oak and hickory. The main **conifer** is loblolly pine.

THE STATE TREE

The Wye Oak, located at Wye Mills in Talbot County, was once the largest white oak tree in the United States. It was about 400 years old in 1941 when the Maryland Assembly voted to make the white oak the state tree. A tiny 29-acre (12 ha) state park surrounded it. But on June 6, 2002, the ancient tree, almost hollowed by age, toppled in a storm. The Linden Oak in North Bethesda is now the largest white oak tree in the United States.

WORD TO KNOW

conifer *an evergreen tree that bears cones and needles instead of leaves*

Blackwater National Wildlife Refuge is a protected home to many native Maryland species.

Residents of Annapolis wade through floodwaters caused by Hurricane Isabel in 2003.

CLIMATE

Because of Maryland's varied topography—from seashore to mountains—it also has a great variety of climates.

The climate around Chesapeake Bay is humid subtropical, meaning that the summers are very hot and humid. Winters are mild and rainy. The region does get some snow, an average of about 10 inches (25 centimeters) per year, but it doesn't stay on the ground long.

Away from Chesapeake Bay and the ocean, Maryland has a continental climate. It

Weather Report

This chart shows record temperatures (high and low) for the state, as well as average temperatures (July and January) and average annual precipitation.

Record high temperature . . . . 109°F (43°C) in Allegany County on July 3, 1898, and at Cumberland and Frederick on July 10, 1936
Record low temperature . . . . –40°F (–40°C) at Oakland on January 13, 1912
Average January temperature . . . . 32°F (0°C)
Average July temperature . . . . 77°F (25°C)
Average yearly precipitation . . . . 41 inches (104 cm)

Source: National Climatic Data Center, NESDIS, NOAA, U.S. Dept. of Commerce

gets the air masses that swoop across the continent, bringing colder winters and less humid summers. The mountain areas may get as much as 110 inches (280 cm) of snow, which lingers all winter. The mountains get the most rain from July through September.

Occasionally, Maryland is struck by a hurricane. In 2003, Hurricane Isabel caused a storm surge (a great movement of water onto land) that destroyed numerous buildings in the bay area.

PROTECTING THE ENVIRONMENT

In the 1970s, the federal Environmental Protection Agency (EPA) did a thorough study of the bay and realized that a vital natural and national treasure was in trouble. The bay was polluted from farming fertilizers, engine oil from boats, and oily runoff from the Bay Bridge. These poisonous chemicals were killing the underwater grasses, which are vital for the health of the animals.

In 1983, Maryland joined Virginia, Pennsylvania, the District of Columbia, and the EPA in an agreement to clean up and protect the bay. In 2000, the same groups renewed their restoration efforts, hoping to complete their work by 2010. In 2007, however, they acknowledged that the end is not in sight. The bay remains in trouble, but Marylanders are committed to preserving the treasure that is so important to their state.

RACHEL CARSON: MOTHER OF THE MODERN ENVIRONMENTAL MOVEMENT

Rachel Carson (1907–1964) was born in Pennsylvania but lived most of her life in Maryland, where she grew to love the sea. Her first best-selling book was *The Sea Around Us*. But it was her 1962 book, *Silent Spring*, that made people aware for the first time that not everything science could do was necessarily good. She pointed out that DDT and other chemicals that were increasing the agricultural yield were also killing birds, insects, and other animals. Carson was one of the first six people inducted into the Ecology Hall of Fame. She was also inducted into the Maryland Women's Hall of Fame.

 Want to know more? See www.rachelcarson.org

READ ABOUT

Maryland's Native Americans used the region's rivers for both transportation and food.

c. 10,000 BCE
Human beings occupy Maryland

▲**c. 1500 BCE**
Oysters become an important food source

c. 1000 BCE
Woodland Indians live in Maryland

C H A P T E R   T W O

FIRST PEOPLE

★

P EOPLE HAVE LIVED IN THE AREA WE NOW KNOW AS MARYLAND FOR AT LEAST 12,000 YEARS. By the end of the ice age, about 1000 BCE, Woodland Indians hunted in the forests and fished in the waters of today's Maryland. Later, Algonquians and a group known as Susquehannocks made their homes in Maryland.

c. 800
Bows and arrows come into use

c. 1300
Algonquians arrive from the Great Lakes

▲1500
Susquehannocks move into Maryland

Algonquians used birch-bark canoes for fishing.

A basket used for catching eel

ALGONQUIANS

The native people known as Algonquians lived along the many rivers and estuaries of Maryland. Their own traditions hold that Algonquian-speaking people arrived in Maryland, probably from the Great Lakes region, about 300 years before the Europeans arrived.

The largest groups of Algonquians in Maryland were the Piscataways on the Western Shore and Nanticokes on the Eastern Shore. Many other groups that are sometimes named in Maryland history were subgroups of these native people. North of the bay—and north of the Algonquians—lived a different people.

Native American Peoples

(Before European Contact)

This map shows the general area of Native American peoples before European settlers arrived.

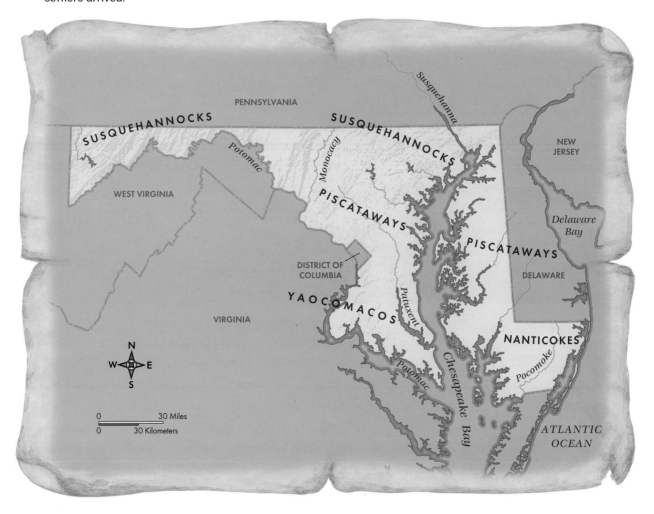

SUSQUEHANNOCKS

North of the Algonquians lived a people who spoke an Iroquoian language. They are known today only as Susquehannocks, meaning "people of the muddy river." The name was given to them by neighboring Algonquian people. These farmers and fishers lived from northern

Susquehannocks lived in longhouses covered with tree bark. Some of the longhouses were large enough for community gatherings.

Maryland up into New York. They lived on their farmlands and in small villages along the Susquehanna River.

Even though they were Iroquoian-speaking people, they were not friends of Iroquois from farther north because they had refused to join the Five Nation Iroquois League, which was probably formed about 1150. From the time they entered the Susquehanna River valley, they were continually at war with their Iroquois relatives. Iroquois gradually drove the Susquehannocks southward, where they, in turn, forced the Algonquian-speaking tribes out of their homes.

Susquehannocks left carvings on the rocks of the rivers they canoed. They wore bear and wolf skins. In addition to bows and arrows, they carried long tobacco pipes and clubs. The men wore their hair long on one side and shaved on the other. Their villages were collections of bark-covered **longhouses** clustered within **palisade** fences.

Little is known about Susquehannocks. Soon after Europeans arrived, most Susquehannocks died from European diseases, or were killed in confrontations with other native groups. There were no Susquehannocks left to tell their tale.

THE ALGONQUIAN CULTURE

The Algonquian people have been recorded as having many different names, usually the names given to the rivers whose shores they occupied.

Algonquians believed that the Great Spirit, who lived where the sun rose, gave them the land and populated it with the animals that shared the land. The animals and everything else around them had spirits, or gods, within them. The people smoked tobacco to cleanse and purify themselves, to make them worthy of communicating with the spirits.

The chief or leader of a village of Algonquians was called a *werowance*. This leader could be male or female. A supreme leader, called a *tayac*, was in charge of a collection of villages.

Shamans, or medicine men, were the spiritual leaders. Through special training, they learned to dance or drum themselves into trances. While in a trance, they could communicate with the spirits, who gave them the ability to heal wounds and cure diseases.

These native people used the forests in many ways. They cut ash trees for bows and alder for arrows. They made tools from hickory, perhaps with beaver teeth for a cutting edge. They cut down and burned out white elm for dugout canoes. They also used logs to make

WORDS TO KNOW

longhouses *long buildings made and used by Native American communities*

palisade *fence of logs set vertically into the ground close to each other to create a protected village*

drums. The women used the thin roots of red cedar for thread to sew deerskins and bark together.

Families lived in homes called **wigwams**. The mats that covered wigwams could be rearranged as needed to protect against chill winds or to let in cooling breezes. Also, a flap around the smoke hole could be moved when the wind direction changed. Cooking was done inside only in the coldest or wettest weather.

Algonquians generally lived in fairly large villages. The different groups gathered at fish spawning grounds. The abundant catch of fish, especially herring and shad, was dried to provide food through the winter.

The people who lived along the Chesapeake harvested oysters simply by walking out into the water and pulling the shelled animals off the bottom. They probably used the shells as money, a means of trade. They must have eaten oysters for many hundreds of years because one pile of oyster shells was found to be 20 feet (6 m) deep and covered about 30 acres (12 ha)!

Algonquians planted corn, beans, and squash in fields that were left untended when they went to the bay during the summer. In the fall, they would return to their fields for harvest. Corn was allowed to dry and then stored for winter.

ALGONQUIAN GROUPS

The most powerful group to take root and grow in Maryland was the Piscataways, who lived along the Potomac River in permanent villages. Piscataways were named after their main village, which was located in what is now Prince George's County. There were probably about 30 Piscataway settlements through-

A wooden needle used for making fishing nets

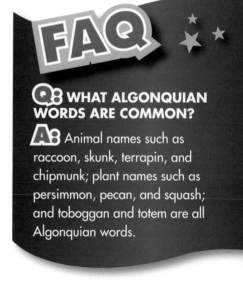

out central Maryland. The Yaocomaco people of the southern part of the Western Shore were related.

The Nanticokes on the Eastern Shore are related to the Lenni-Lenapes, known to Europeans as the Delaware people. Their name is a derivative of Nentego, meaning "tidewater people." Nanticokes were known by other tribes as wizards, thought to possess terrible secrets. This was probably because they grew certain vegetables for their poison content. They also collected the starchy roots of tuckahoe, or arrow arum, which grew in freshwater marshes. They dried the roots and ground them into flour.

Related to Nanticokes were the people called Assateagues. The barrier island on which they lived extends down into Virginia. They were probably part of the Powhatan **Confederation** of Virginia. Powhatans were a group of Algonquians whom the first Europeans found when they came into Virginia. When the Europeans arrived in Chesapeake Bay, everything changed for Maryland's native people.

Algonquians built wigwams from branches and bark.

FAQ

Q8 WHAT ALGONQUIAN WORDS ARE COMMON?

A8 Animal names such as raccoon, skunk, terrapin, and chipmunk; plant names such as persimmon, pecan, and squash; and toboggan and totem are all Algonquian words.

WORD TO KNOW

confederation *an association of groups that come together with common goals*

1498

The land around
Chesapeake Bay is
claimed for England

1608 ▶

John Smith of
Virginia explores
the bay

1634

The first colonists
arrive aboard the
Ark *and the* Dove

CHAPTER THREE

EXPLORATION AND SETTLEMENT

★

IN 1498, ON THE BASIS OF SIGHTINGS BY BRITISH EXPLORER JOHN CABOT, ENGLAND CLAIMED THE LAND AROUND CHESAPEAKE BAY. In 1524, the king of France sent Italian navigator Giovanni da Verrazzano to investigate the area. He reached Chesapeake Bay, but did not sail into it. To prove he had been there, however, Verrazzano kidnapped an Assateague child and took him back to France.

1694
The capital
is moved to
Annapolis

◀**1774**
Marylanders burn the
British ship the *Peggy*
Stewart

▲**1788**
Maryland becomes
the seventh state

GEORGE CALVERT: THE MAN WITH A DREAM

George Calvert (c. 1580–1632) worked for Britain's King James I. When he served in Ireland, the king gave him lands. Calvert converted to Catholicism while he was there, but because Catholics were not allowed to serve in high offices, he had to resign his post. The king still honored him by granting him the title Baron of Baltimore, the name of a small Irish town.

Lord Baltimore invested in the colonization companies of Virginia and New England. But he wanted to begin a colony that would welcome both Catholics and Protestants. He bought land in Newfoundland and led some settlers there. Finding he disliked the cold, he asked King Charles I for a land grant just north of Virginia, on the other side of the Potomac River. Before the king could grant his request, Lord Baltimore died. The king granted a charter for the Province of Maryland to George Calvert's son, Cecil, the second Lord Baltimore, on June 20, 1632.

Want to know more? See http://www.heritage.nf.ca/exploration/avalon.html

FAQ

Q8 WHICH EUROPEAN EXPLORER REACHED MARYLAND FIRST?

A8 It's possible that a Viking explorer named Thorfinn Karlsfennias sailed into Chesapeake Bay as early as the 11th century.

EXPLORING THE BAY

In 1572, Spain's Pedro Menéndez de Avilés was probably the first European explorer to enter Chesapeake Bay. When Spanish missionaries were killed by the Powhatan in Virginia, Avilés executed some Native people as revenge. That act kept the Native people from ever trusting the Spanish. Eventually, Spain gave up on claiming the northern regions and concentrated on Florida and the Carolinas.

Things were quiet for the Native people in Maryland until 1608, when English captain John Smith explored the bay. He had helped the Virginia Company plan its colonization of Virginia and was one of the leaders at Jamestown. Smith was captured by Native Americans and held by the Powhatan chief for a month. The chief released Smith, according to one story, at the urging of his young daughter, Pocahontas.

Smith found that his colonists had made no effort to build a permanent colony in his absence. He decided to explore. Sailing to the north end of Chesapeake Bay,

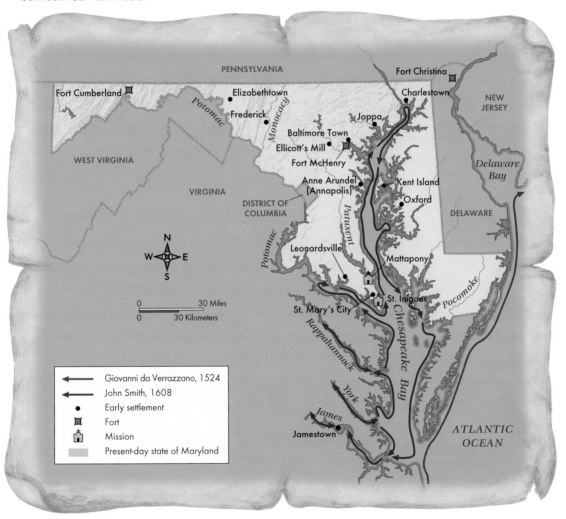

European Exploration of Maryland

The colored arrows on this map show the routes taken by explorers between 1524 and 1608.

Map labels:

PENNSYLVANIA

Fort Cumberland

Elizabethtown

Frederick

WEST VIRGINIA

Potomac

Monocacy

Baltimore Town

Ellicott's Mill

Fort McHenry

Anne Arundel (Annapolis)

VIRGINIA

DISTRICT OF COLUMBIA

Joppa

Fort Christina

Charlestown

NEW JERSEY

Kent Island

Oxford

Delaware Bay

DELAWARE

Patuxent

Potomac

Leonardsville

Mattapony

St. Inigoes

St. Mary's City

Chesapeake Bay

Pocomoke

Rappahannock

York

James

Jamestown

ATLANTIC OCEAN

Legend:
- Giovanni da Verrazzano, 1524
- John Smith, 1608
- • Early settlement
- Fort
- Mission
- Present-day state of Maryland

he ventured into the Susquehanna River, and met some Native people. Smith described the area around Chesapeake Bay as "the most pleasant place ever knowne [sic]." Ever since, "Land of Pleasant Living" has been one of Maryland's nicknames.

MAKING A COLONY

The charter given by King Charles I to Cecil Calvert, the second Lord Baltimore, made him the proprietor, or owner of the colony. This meant he could do whatever he wanted with it. Baltimore wanted to turn Maryland into a business, to deal properly with Native people, and to grow cash crops such as tobacco, which had become popular in Europe. He also wanted to make his colony a place of religious tolerance.

On a crisp March day in 1634, Native Americans, probably Yaocomacos, a band of Piscataways, gathered on the banks of the Potomac to watch the approach of two strange ships. Seeing the waiting people and not knowing what to expect, the sailors stopped at an island they called St. Clements. On board the *Ark* and the *Dove* were about 150 men and women, both Catholics and Protestants. The men had been chosen for being of "good birth and qualitie." They had all been promised land by Lord Baltimore. The **indentured servants** of these men also acquired land after working out their indenture time.

The British found a Native American interpreter in Virginia. He helped their leader, Leonard Calvert, Lord Baltimore's brother and the first governor of Maryland, negotiate with a Yaocomaco chieftain to purchase an abandoned village. The colonists surrounded the village with a protective palisade and called it St. Mary's City. When the legislature, called the assembly, started meeting there in 1635, it became Maryland's first capital.

Two priests who had been aboard the *Ark* and *Dove*, Father Andrew White and Father John Altham, held a religious service with an altar set up in a wigwam. They decided to learn the American Indian languages and even created a dictionary of the Piscataway language.

Father Andrew White met with Native Americans and told them of his Christian religion.

MEETING THE PISCATAWAY

Father Andrew White described the first meeting of the colonists with Piscataways. "All were heer armed: 500 Bow-men came to the Water-side. The Emperour himself more fearelesse than the rest, came privately aboord, where hee was courteously entertained; and understanding wee came in a peaceable manner, bade us welcome, and gave us leave to sit down in what place of his kingdome wee pleased."

When the colonists felt safe from attack, they moved beyond their village and began to establish manors and farms, using the land Lord Baltimore had granted them. Many took over fields previously used by Native people, and others cleared trees.

Back in England, a civil war was waging between royalists, who supported Catholic Charles I, and Parliament, which was Protestant. The members of Parliament insisted that, as king, Charles did not have the divine, or God-given, right to do whatever he wanted, especially to raise taxes. In 1645, Richard Ingle, a Protestant sea captain, and his men plundered the Maryland Colony and drove out the Catholics or imprisoned them. Leonard Calvert

MARGARET BRENT: EARLY COLONIST

Margaret Brent (ca. 1601–1671) arrived in Maryland in 1638 with her brothers and sister from Gloucestershire in England and settled on land given to them by Lord Baltimore. Margaret and her sister, Mary, invested in the businesses of newcomers to the colony.

As he lay dying, Leonard Calvert made Margaret Brent the executor of his estate, giving her charge of all his wealth. The Maryland Assembly also made her Lord Baltimore's attorney so that she could sell some of his Maryland assets. The sale of these assets saved the Maryland Colony from financial collapse. Brent is a member of the Maryland Women's Hall of Fame.

Want to know more? See http://www.msa.md.gov/msa/speccol/sc3500/sc3520/002100/002177/html/brochure.html

WORD TO KNOW

indigenous *native to a certain place*

fled to Virginia. He returned in a few months with troops who took over the seriously weakened colony again. Ingle was executed, and Calvert died a few months later.

Colonists and Native People

European settlers had occupied Virginia since 1607. In 1622, many settlers were killed in a war with the Powhatan Confederacy. Angry Virginians began to roam far and wide, killing Indians. These vicious attacks sometimes carried them into what would become Maryland.

The earliest Marylanders had established friendships with various Algonquian villages, but war was never far away. From 1630 to 1700, the Native groups of Maryland were caught up in the Beaver Wars, battles between villages, encouraged by Europeans. But the worst European threat to Native Americans was disease. The Europeans brought diseases previously unknown in North America, such as smallpox, which struck down thousands of Native people, especially Susquehannocks.

The Maryland Assembly established the earliest Native American reservations in America when they decreed that certain lands on the Eastern Shore could be used only by Native nations. As the colony grew, however, these lands became more attractive to European settlers, and Native Americans lost again.

Edward Scarborough of Virginia was determined to rid the Delmarva Peninsula of its **indigenous** people.

The officials of the Maryland Colony refused to help him, but he succeeded in forcing six groups of Assateagues to resettle at today's Snow Hill. People from the Assateague, Pocomoke, and several other small groups established Indian Town.

In 1706, the remaining Susquehannocks were allowed to build their own village along the Susquehanna River. One by one, though, they died from disease or war wounds. The last 20 or so Susquehannock survivors were slaughtered in 1763 by a mob of colonists.

In 1742, Nanticokes along the Pocomoke River developed a plan to kill the settlers. A Choptank American Indian informed the settlers, who then threatened to take all Native land. Most of the Nanticokes went north to live with Iroquois. Others eventually settled in Delaware.

Citizens of African Descent

Mathias de Sousa served his indenture time and became free, and in 1642, he was elected to the assembly. That same year, Governor Leonard Calvert bought 17 enslaved Africans. They were put to work in Maryland's farm fields. Eventually, the Eastern Shore became an agricultural area supported completely by slave labor.

In 1664, the Maryland Assembly passed the first colonial law that enslaved Africans for life. At the same time, a Maryland law stated that any white woman who married an African slave also had to become a slave for life.

Religious Arguments

In England, the struggles between Catholics and Protestants were continuing. Lord Baltimore, still aiming for religious freedom, encouraged more Protestants to settle in his colony. Then in 1649, the assembly voted

Mathias de Sousa

W★W

Mathias de Sousa was the first person of African heritage in Maryland. A servant indentured to Father Andrew White, de Sousa was aboard the *Ark* when it arrived in 1634.

Picture Yourself . . .

as a Slave in Maryland

As soon as you were old enough to understand directions, you had to help in the slaves' gardens or care for a sheep or cow. All too soon, you were sent into the fields to carry water or run errands. By the time you were eight, you were expected to put in a full day's hard labor in the tobacco fields. And a full day might be 14 or more hours.

On any day, whether you worked in the house or outside, you might be sold to another plantation far away. You would never see any of your family or friends again. As you grew up, you realized that your life would not get better.

to pass the Act of Toleration. This law granted all citizens the right to practice whatever religion they chose, as long as it was a form of Christianity.

After that law was passed, some Puritans moved to Maryland from Virginia. This was to protest the Church of England being declared the official church of the Virginia Colony. Lord Baltimore offered Puritans land on the Severn River, and the settlement of Providence quickly drew 25,000 residents. By 1694, it became the capital and its name was changed to Annapolis.

Friction grew between Catholics loyal to Lord Baltimore and Protestants loyal to the British crown. In 1689, John Coode led a rebellion of Protestants against Maryland Catholics who had not recognized the new Protestant king and queen in England. A Protestant army forced the assembly to surrender its power. England's Queen Mary made Maryland a royal colony, though she did not take away Lord Baltimore's proprietary rights. Despite his dream of Maryland as a place of religious liberty, the Protestants made the Church of England the official state church.

Maryland remained a royal colony for 25 years until, back in England, the fourth Lord Baltimore converted to Protestantism. The queen returned control of the colony to him as proprietor, and the Maryland Assembly took away the rights of Catholics to vote and hold office.

LEADING TO REVOLUTION

Maryland's earliest cities were established along Chesapeake Bay, especially on the Eastern Shore.

Fort Cumberland, Maryland, in 1755

Cambridge was founded in 1669, Oxford in 1683, and Easton in 1692. It wasn't until Baltimore was founded in 1729 that Maryland's people began to migrate toward the western part of Lord Baltimore's colony.

In the 1750s, Britain had an ongoing war with France that soon inflamed the Americas. British troops were sent to the western frontiers of the colonies. British general Edward Braddock's troops built Fort Cumberland at the western end of the Maryland colony. After Braddock was killed in battle, a young soldier in the Virginia militia named George Washington led Braddock's troops back to Fort Cumberland.

Called the French and Indian War in America, it ended in favor of the British. The French lost Canada and their fur-trapping lands to the British. Washington's experience in the war helped him become a leader in the American Revolution and led to his becoming the

The Burning of the Peggy Stewart by Francis Blackwell Mayer, painted in 1896

WORD TO KNOW

boycott *the organized refusal to use a service or buy a product, as a form of protest*

nation's first commander in chief.

After the French and Indian War, the British government wanted colonists to pay for the war's expenses and keep British troops on the western frontiers. In 1764, the British government imposed new taxes on the colonies. Many of the colonists began to rebel. They said no taxes could be imposed without the colonies being represented in Parliament.

Revolution was in the air. Some Marylanders formed protest groups and called themselves the Sons of Liberty. One protest method was to **boycott** British goods. The colonists knew such an action would hurt the British economy. In 1769, Baltimore and Annapolis shopkeepers joined a boycott that had started in New England. The boycott worked. All taxes were removed—except for those on tea.

In protest, colonists in Boston, Massachusetts, dressed as Native Americans and boarded a British merchant ship. Then they dumped a cargo of tea into the harbor. This became known as the Boston Tea Party.

Marylanders did the same—twice. First, Chester Town held its own tea party on May 23, 1774, five months after the Boston event. The residents voted to not import, sell, or use tea. They climbed aboard a ship in the Chester River and threw its tea overboard. Then, on October 19, 1774, in Annapolis, Marylanders burned the British ship *Peggy Stewart* and its 2,000 pounds (907 kilograms) of tea.

After the Boston Tea Party, the British closed Boston Harbor and placed the Massachusetts Colony under military rule. Marylanders now were ready to join other colonists in a protest meeting in Philadelphia. Only Georgia failed to send representatives to what later was called the First Continental Congress. It met just long enough to agree to continue the boycott and to plan a second meeting for the spring of 1775.

By the time the Second Continental Congress met in 1775, warfare had erupted in Massachusetts. Delegates knew they could no longer just talk, they had to act. They chose George Washington of Virginia to command an army. They were still hoping that the British king, George III, would compromise. Instead, he called the colonists traitors. They believed they were patriots, loyal to their new country, and they were ready to take a stand against their mother country.

The Continental Congress asked Thomas Jefferson to draft a statement declaring the independence of the colonies from Great Britain. The delegates agreed that all should sign it. When Maryland's four delegates signed it, what had been a colony became part of a new country.

EARLY NEWSPAPER PUBLISHERS

Siblings William (1740–1817) and Mary Katherine (1738–1816) Goddard started Baltimore's first newspaper in 1773. William had been publishing the *Pennsylvania Chronicle* for several years. When he published news sympathetic to the Revolution, the royal postal carriers refused to deliver it. William designed a postal system that would be free from governmental interference, and in 1774 he presented his plan to the Continental Congress. It was adopted the next year. Benjamin Franklin became the first postmaster general, and he made Mary Katherine the postmistress of Baltimore, a position she held for 14 years.

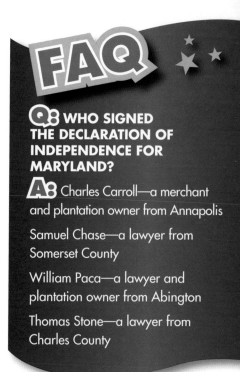

FAQ

Q8 WHO SIGNED THE DECLARATION OF INDEPENDENCE FOR MARYLAND?

A8 Charles Carroll—a merchant and plantation owner from Annapolis

Samuel Chase—a lawyer from Somerset County

William Paca—a lawyer and plantation owner from Abington

Thomas Stone—a lawyer from Charles County

A NEW NICKNAME FOR MARYLAND

Marylanders fought throughout the American Revolution. But one day in particular gave the state its best-known nickname. The Battle of Long Island, the first major battle of the war, was fought on August 27, 1776, in New York. The Maryland Line, consisting of about 400 men, held off thousands of enemy troops while others in the Continental army made their way through a swamp. George Washington was said to have praised the steadfast Maryland Line, and Maryland became the "Old Line State."

Many German immigrants had moved to western Maryland, along the frontier. They formed a regiment of their own, fought in several battles, and spent the harsh winter of 1777 with Washington at Valley Forge, Pennsylvania. General Casimir Pulaski, a Polish officer, served under Washington. Using Baltimore as his headquarters, he formed the first American cavalry unit and recruited many immigrants from Poland, Ireland, France, and Germany.

Soon after the war was over, Annapolis became the only state capital to serve as the capital of the United States. The Continental Congress met in Annapolis from November 26, 1783, to June 3, 1784. During this session of the congress two notable events took place. George Washington resigned as commander in chief of the Continental Army and the Treaty of Paris was ratified.

THE NEW GOVERNMENT

Congress's greatest task was to create a government for the new country. The result was called the Articles of Confederation. John Hanson of Charles County is sometimes called the first president of the United States because he was president of the Congress, the legislature created by the Articles of Confederation.

In this plan, most power remained in the hands of the individual states. The federal government had little power to make decisions. During three months in 1787, a congress of states created a new plan and a document called the Constitution of the United States. Small states wanted to have as much power as big states, and big states thought they should have more. James Madison suggested two legislative houses, one based on states' populations and one with the same number of representatives for each state. But the slavery issue was not solved.

On April 28, 1788, the Maryland legislature voted to approve, or **ratify**, the new Constitution. Maryland then gained another of its nicknames: the Seventh State.

Maryland: From Territory to Statehood
(1632–1788)

This map shows the original Maryland territory and the area (outlined in yellow) that became the state of Maryland in 1788.

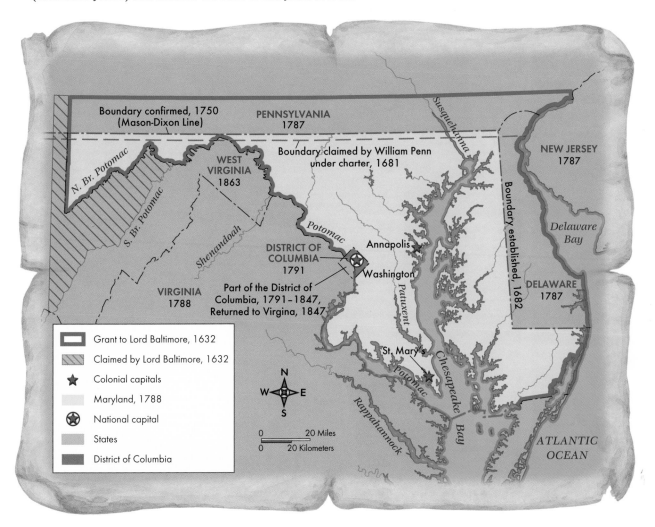

Boundary confirmed, 1750 (Mason-Dixon Line)

PENNSYLVANIA 1787

Boundary claimed by William Penn under charter, 1681

Susquehanna

NEW JERSEY 1787

N. Br. Potomac

WEST VIRGINIA 1863

S. Br. Potomac

Shenandoah

Potomac

Boundary established, 1682

Delaware Bay

DISTRICT OF COLUMBIA 1791

Annapolis

Washington

DELAWARE 1787

VIRGINIA 1788

Part of the District of Columbia, 1791–1847, Returned to Virginia, 1847

Patuxent

St. Mary's

Chesapeake Bay

Potomac

Rappahannock

ATLANTIC OCEAN

Legend:
- Grant to Lord Baltimore, 1632
- Claimed by Lord Baltimore, 1632
- ★ Colonial capitals
- Maryland, 1788
- ⊛ National capital
- States
- District of Columbia

N W E S

0   20 Miles
0   20 Kilometers

READ ABOUT

The capital city of Washington, D.C., was built on land donated by Maryland. Here, the dome on the U.S. Capitol is completed in 1863.

1812–1815 ▲
The War of 1812 is fought

1818
The Cumberland Road to the West opens

1829
Chesapeake and Delaware Canal is built

CHAPTER FOUR

GROWTH AND CHANGE

★

IN 1791, GEORGE WASHINGTON SELECTED A PARCEL OF LAND THAT MARYLAND WOULD DONATE TO BE USED AS A CAPITAL CITY FOR THE NEW FEDERAL GOVERNMENT. Washington, D.C., the new nation's capital, was between the North and the South, on land that would belong to the entire country.

▲ **1838**
Frederick Douglass escapes from slavery in Baltimore

▲ **1862**
Battle of Antietam, the Civil War's deadliest battle, is fought

1904
Downtown Baltimore burns

THE EARLY DAYS OF STATEHOOD

The young nation was just settling down when the United States began to fear the possibility of a war with France. Maryland built a fort on an island in the river off Baltimore to protect that vital city. Called Fort McHenry, it wasn't needed then, but it would be later, in a different war, with a familiar enemy—Great Britain.

THE WAR OF 1812

European nations were at war with the French forces of Napoleon Bonaparte for many years at the start of the 19th century. Frequently, American sailors were kidnapped and forced to serve on British ships. This illegal action made Americans angry, as did Britain's failure to leave the frontier territory it had surrendered to the United States at the end of the Revolutionary War.

The War of 1812, which lasted into 1815, was fought in the Great Lakes region and Canada. Americans burned the Canadian city of York (now Toronto), and the British planned to retaliate by invading the new capital, Washington, D.C.

British forces sailed into Chesapeake Bay and landed at Benedict. Then troops advanced toward Washington and quickly outgunned Maryland troops in the three-hour Battle of Bladensburg. The British soldiers headed toward Washington and burned government buildings, including the unfinished president's mansion. The jubilant British troops then sailed up the bay toward Baltimore. Almost 5,000 British troops landed in the early morning of September 12, 1814, but were stopped by a garrison of Maryland soldiers at Fort McHenry. After two days of fighting, the British decided to wait for reinforcements. September 12 is celebrated as Defenders Day in Maryland.

THE FLAG STILL FLEW

On the night of September 13–14, 1814, 19 British ships in Baltimore Harbor shelled Fort McHenry (left) with rockets. But the next morning, they could see that even after the massive shelling, the U.S. flag still flew over the fort. Lawyer Francis Scott Key, who was watching the action from a boat in the harbor, wrote a poem commemorating the event. His poem became "The Star-Spangled Banner." The actual flag, made by Baltimore businesswoman Mary Pickersgill, hangs, tattered and torn, in the National Museum of American History in Washington, D.C. Key's poem was later set to music and adopted as the national anthem on March 3, 1931.

EXPANDING FROM BALTIMORE

Baltimore quickly became the center of Maryland's economic activity and was soon the second-largest city in the country. Industry built up along the river and bay. The city looked for ways to compete with New York.

For almost 200 years, the only way for a boat to get from the Chesapeake Bay to the Atlantic Ocean was to make the 200-mile (322-km) trip to the mouth of the bay. After several attempts to get it built, a canal, with numerous **locks**, was opened to traffic in 1829. It runs across the Eastern Shore between Chesapeake City and Delaware Bay. It connects two major cities—Baltimore and Philadelphia. The Chesapeake and Delaware Canal was bought by the federal government in 1919. It was widened twice and made deeper to eliminate the locks.

WORD TO KNOW

locks *devices on a waterway for raising or lowering a boat by changing the level of the water*

SEE IT HERE!

HISTORIC TRAIN TERMINAL

The Baltimore & Ohio Railroad built what is now the oldest railroad terminal in the country at Mount Clare, in the 1830s. The nation's first regularly scheduled passenger train traveled from Mount Clare to Ellicott Mills. On May 24, 1844, Samuel Morse used his newly developed code of electrical dots and dashes to send the nation's first telegraph message. It passed through the railroad station to Morse's partner in Baltimore. His message, chosen by the daughter of a friend, was "What hath God wrought?" The terminal, containing a replica of the train the *Tom Thumb*, is now a museum run by the National Park Service.

Today, the canal is 14 miles (22.5 km) long and 450 feet (137 m) wide. Millions of tons of cargo are moved through it every year.

The Baltimore & Ohio Railroad was under construction at the same time as the canal. Its first track was only 13 miles (21 km) long, but when it opened for service in 1830, it became the first regular railway service in the country.

SLAVERY

Slavery had long been an issue between Northern and Southern states, especially after the Northern states outlawed it. Maryland, as a border state, had some residents who wanted to keep slavery and others

A Baltimore & Ohio Railroad locomotive in 1848

Enslaved African Americans were aided along the Underground Railroad to freedom in the North and in Canada.

BUYING FREEDOM WITH INVENTION

Born into slavery in about 1830, Benjamin Bradley bought his own freedom with money he earned from an invention. As a teenager, he made a working steam engine out of bits of scrap metal. He impressed the right people, because he was given a job at the U.S. Naval Academy in Annapolis, where he created science-experiment setups for professors. He earned little, though, because his wages went to his master. He used what he could save to buy materials to make a steam engine big enough to power a ship. As an enslaved man, he could not get a patent on his invention, but he earned enough money to buy his own freedom.

WORD TO KNOW

abolition *the act of ending slavery through the passage of laws*

who believed in **abolition**. William Lloyd Garrison was an important leader of the abolition movement who published a journal called the *Liberator*. He soon had the support of an outspoken former slave from Maryland, Frederick Douglass.

Maryland played a crucial role in the battle for liberty in the United States. Maryland's east coast, close to Pennsylvania and New Jersey, became a leading corridor on the Underground Railroad. This was a series of safe places for escaped slaves to stay as they sought freedom in the North and Canada. Brave conductors on the Underground Railroad secretly moved frightened men, women, and children across fields, over streams, and along deserted roads.

President Abraham Lincoln, along with General George McClellan (sixth from the left), visits the Antietam battlefield.

WORD TO KNOW

secede *to withdraw from a group or organization*

and write. The state even had six private schools for African American children.

The issue of slavery and its extension to the West led to war between Northern states, where slavery had been abolished, and 11 Southern slave states. In December 1860, the Southern states began to break away, or **secede**, from the United States to form their own nation, the Confederate States of America.

In Maryland, military actions began on April 19, 1861, when a Massachusetts regiment marched through Baltimore and was attacked by a pro-Confederate mob. Four soldiers and 12 civilians were killed. Three days later, Union troops took possession of Annapolis. The next month, Union troops occupied Baltimore. These moves kept Maryland slaveholders from leading Maryland into secession. If Maryland had seceded, Washington, D.C., would have been surrounded by Confederate states.

Maryland's governor called a special session of the General Assembly. He knew that if it met in Annapolis, which was occupied by federal troops, anti-Union forces would prevail. So he arranged to meet in Frederick, which was a pro-Union city. The assembly met throughout the summer of 1861. Several bills were introduced to link Maryland with the Confederacy, but they all failed to pass. Pro-Union forces managed to keep Maryland neutral.

Baltimore remained under Union military control throughout the war. Eventually, 22,000 Marylanders fought in the Confederate army (mostly from the Eastern Shore) and 62,000, including many African Americans, fought in the Union army.

THE DEADLIEST BATTLE

The Battle of Antietam (called Sharpsburg in the South) took place between the Union's Army of the Potomac, under Major General George B. McClellan, and the Confederate Army of Northern Virginia under General Robert E. Lee. On September 17, 1862, Lee brought his troops into Maryland from Virginia, in an attempt to encircle and capture the capital at Washington. Because Maryland was a slaveholding state, he also hoped to find new recruits there.

On that one day, in what was the first battle on Northern territory, nearly 23,000 Union and Confederate soldiers were killed or wounded. It was the bloodiest battle to take place on a single day in U.S. history.

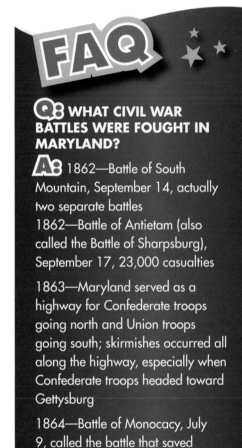

FAQ

Q8 WHAT CIVIL WAR BATTLES WERE FOUGHT IN MARYLAND?

A8 1862—Battle of South Mountain, September 14, actually two separate battles

1862—Battle of Antietam (also called the Battle of Sharpsburg), September 17, 23,000 casualties

1863—Maryland served as a highway for Confederate troops going north and Union troops going south; skirmishes occurred all along the highway, especially when Confederate troops headed toward Gettysburg

1864—Battle of Monocacy, July 9, called the battle that saved Washington, D.C.

MINI-BIO

ISAAC MYERS: LABOR LEADER

Isaac Myers (1835–1891) was born to free blacks in Baltimore. He acquired an education, and as a teenager he went to work in the shipyards. At the end of the Civil War, white workers drove African American laborers out of the shipyards. Myers and black and white investors formed their own shipping and dry dock company in Fells Point. In 1869, he started the Colored National Labor Union (CNLU), the first major organization of African American workers. Its success forced the white National Labor Union to accept black members. When an economic depression killed the CNLU, he started another union that fought for equal rights. In 2006, to bring the shipping area's history to life, the Frederick Douglass–Isaac Myers Maritime Park was opened in Fells Point.

? Want to know more?
See www.mdoe.org/myersisaac.html

RECONSTRUCTION IN MARYLAND

Maryland's white voters passed a new constitution in September 1864. It not only ended slavery but established the first tax-supported public school system. But it did not establish any schools for black children. It also gave increased political power to nonslaveholding whites and denied the vote to African Americans, who accounted for 20 percent of the population. It also allowed the apprenticeship of black children, over the objections of their parents.

Then in 1867, another constitution handed power back to wealthy plantation counties in the South. A white critic said this meant "the right of a few white men, by counting disenfranchised blacks, to govern a great many white men. This is progress backwards."

Finally, in 1870, the Fifteenth Amendment to the U.S. Constitution was ratified and the vote was extended to all men.

WHEN BALTIMORE BURNED

On the night of February 7, 1904, a fire in a factory exploded through the building's roof before the fire department could arrive. The fire quickly spread to other buildings. Within minutes more help from Washington was called. But when District firemen arrived, they found that their hoses didn't fit the hydrants properly. Dynamite was used to keep the fire from reaching unburned buildings, but it didn't work. The wind increased throughout the day and night, and it often changed direction. Fire companies came from miles away. Twenty-seven hours later, the main fires were out, but many of Baltimore's buildings smoldered for weeks. Seventy square blocks had burned to the ground. Only 10 downtown structures survived the Great Baltimore Fire. Amazingly, only one person died.

By the late 1800s, the people of Maryland saw many changes, including growing industry, new schools, and expanding cities.

GROWING BALTIMORE

With the end of the Civil War, immigrants by the thousands moved into the Baltimore area, especially from Germany. Many of them immediately took the trains west, but others stayed to work along Chesapeake Bay. They helped build a huge canning industry that sent the bounty of the bay to the western states. Railroads expanded, and the Eastern Shore gradually became more accessible. By the turn of the 20th century, more than half of Maryland's people lived in Baltimore.

Another industry that contributed to Baltimore's growth was shipbuilding. Baltimore had been turning out ships almost since the city was founded. Congress had acquired the first U.S. naval vessel, the USS *Constellation*, from Baltimore. A Civil War vessel also called the *Constellation*, built in 1854, can still be seen docked at Pier 1 in Baltimore.

When the United States entered World War I in 1917, Baltimore's ships played an important role in the fight against Germany. The federal government also used some of Maryland's open spaces for new facilities. Fort Meade was built in Anne Arundel County. Aberdeen Proving Ground, for weapons testing, opened along the marshy bay shore. Both of these facilities, which opened in 1917, are still in use. Fort McHenry was reopened as a military hospital that same year. In 1925, when it was no longer needed, Fort McHenry became a national park.

MINI-BIO

MATTHEW HENSON: FIRST TO REACH THE NORTH POLE

Matthew Henson (1866–1955), an African American child orphaned at an early age, yearned to read more and to travel far from his Baltimore home. As a cabin boy on ships, he sailed the Pacific and Atlantic oceans and the Baltic Sea by the time he was 18. In 1887, he met explorer Robert Peary and soon became a valuable member of Peary's exploration team.

Their most famous exploration took the men to the Arctic. On April 6, 1909, they succeeded in reaching the North Pole. Henson actually arrived at the North Pole more than a half hour before Peary, but Peary insisted on taking all the credit. He ordered Henson never to discuss it in public. Though others would say that Peary was the first person to reach the North Pole, Henson knew the truth. The first man there was an orphan boy from Baltimore who loved adventure and books.

? Want to know more? See http://news.national geographic.com/news/2003/01/0110_030113_henson.html

1937

The town of
Greenbelt is built

1941

The United States
enters World War II

▲**1952**

The Bay Bridge gives
access to the Eastern
Shore

CHAPTER FIVE

MORE MODERN TIMES

★

FOLLOWING WORLD WAR I, MANY THINGS BEGAN TO CHANGE RAPIDLY IN MARYLAND, AS THEY DID ELSE-WHERE IN THE UNITED STATES. Women were given the right to vote, and they first exercised that right in Maryland in 1920. Baltimore acquired both a symphony orchestra and a great museum of art. All children were required to go to school. But change of a different kind was coming.

1967
Race riots take place in Cambridge

▲ **1981**
The National Aquarium opens in Baltimore

2007
Maryland enacts the "living wage" law

THE GREAT DEPRESSION

In the years after World War I, Maryland, the nation, and the rest of the world were plunged into a period of economic disaster that lasted through the 1930s. After the stock market collapsed in October 1929, businesses closed, people lost their savings and homes, and the monetary crisis extended internationally. The Great Depression resulted in massive unemployment, not only in Maryland but across the entire nation. Many Americans fell into poverty.

President Franklin D. Roosevelt sought to improve conditions for Americans by beginning a program of relief, reform, and recovery known as the New Deal. One of his new agencies, the Resettlement Administration, moved people from places of poverty and little hope to new cities. Those eligible included farmers with unworkable land, who were relocated to places where they could earn a living.

Many new cities were planned by this agency, but only three—in Maryland, Wisconsin, and Ohio—were actually built. Greenbelt, Maryland's new town, rose up over old, overworked tobacco fields near the Potomac River, only 11 miles (18 km) from Washington, D.C. Its first residents arrived in 1937. They were poor and from a mix of religious backgrounds.

In keeping with attitudes common at the time, all of the town's residents were white. The houses the people were offered included only town houses. Later, single-family houses went up in some of the neighbor-hoods. After World War II, the government sold the housing units, and Greenbelt became a regular town. Today, it is home to about 22,000 people of many different economic levels and of quite varied ethnicities. NASA's Goddard Space Flight Center is located there.

WORLD WAR II

The battleship USS *Maryland* was among the ships anchored at Pearl Harbor, Hawai'i, when it was bombed by Japan on December 7, 1941. The *Maryland* took two direct hits but later returned to fight again in the Pacific. The attack on Pearl Harbor brought the United States into World War II.

Jobs that disappeared during the Depression came back when the war started. Baltimore industries were hiring people by the thousands, especially those who could build ships. The government's New Deal agencies began expanding, too. And as men went off to war, women took their places in industry.

WORLD WAR II MANUFACTURING

Bethlehem-Fairfield Shipyard in Baltimore made the first Liberty ship, *Patrick Henry*, in 1941. Liberty ships were designed to be built quickly and cheaply for transporting cargo to Europe during World War II. Eventually, 385 of the 2,700 Liberty ships were built in Maryland. One of only two still in use is stationed in Baltimore. The Glenn L. Martin Company, also in Baltimore, built thousands of aircraft used in the war. They were mostly bombers, including the famed B-26 Marauder.

Women worked as arc welders at the Bethlehem-Fairfield shipyards in Baltimore during World War II.

National Guard troops attempt to control University of Maryland students protesting the Vietnam War in 1971.

WOW

The 50-star U.S. flag, incorporating stars for the new states of Hawai'i and Alaska, was first officially raised on July 4, 1960, at Fort McHenry.

Nixon chose him as his vice presidential running mate. They won the election, but Agnew was forced to resign in 1973 for having failed to pay taxes on money he had received illegally.

As the civil rights movement gained momentum, another city was rising in central Maryland, in Howard County, halfway between Washington and Baltimore. Like Greenbelt, Columbia was a planned city. It was created by James W. Rouse as an integrated community. Rouse's plan called for residents to live in 10 villages that felt like friendly small towns. Columbia opened in 1967, and today is home to more than 90,000 people. About 65 percent of them are white and just under 25 percent are

African American. Hispanics and other groups make up about 10 percent of Columbia's residents.

In the 1960s and 1970s, some Marylanders fought in the Vietnam War, while others protested it. Catonsville, a suburb of Baltimore, became famous in 1968 when nine Catholic men and women took military **draft** records and burned in them in a parking lot. Arrested and convicted, the group became known as the Catonsville Nine. They all served short terms in prison. The most famous of the nine, Father Daniel Berrigan, later wrote a play called *The Trial of the Catonsville Nine*.

REBUILDING BALTIMORE

In 1950, Baltimore was the sixth-largest city in the country, primarily because of steel manufacturing. Steel had been made at Sparrows Point since the 1880s, and the factory employed immigrant Finns, Czechs, Italians, Lithuanians, and others. After 1950, however, steelmaking and other manufacturing declined dramatically. More than one-third of Baltimore's residents moved out of the city. The population of the suburbs surrounding the city grew from about 400,000 in 1950 to 1.8 million in the 1990s. By 2007, Baltimore was the 19th-largest city in the country.

To revitalize Baltimore, the Inner Harbor waterfront area was rehabilitated. Condominiums were built, bringing residents back to the city. Cuts in property taxes also made a difference. The population has not fallen since 2000, and projections call for it to rise again starting in 2008.

INTERNATIONAL INVOLVEMENT

Camp David is a presidential retreat located in Maryland's Catoctin Mountains. It has been the location of several important meetings in the long and complicated quest for peace in the Middle East, where Arabs and Israelis have struggled since Israel was declared a nation in 1948.

In 1978, President Jimmy Carter arranged a meeting between Egypt's president Anwar Sadat and Israel's prime minister Menachem Begin. The historic meetings led to the Camp David Accords, a peace agreement between those nations in September of that year.

Twenty years later, Maryland again was the location for meetings to move the peace process ahead in the Middle East. A conference was held in 1998 at the Wye River Conference Center in Queenstown. President Bill Clinton brought together Israel's prime minister Benjamin Netanyahu and Palestinian leader Yasser Arafat. Agreements were reached over land jointly claimed by Palestinians and Israelis.

Baltimore's revitalized Inner Harbor is a popular tourist destination.

The city's fascinating history and its many attractions, both old and new, have made tourism the third-highest moneymaker in "Charm City." Each year, Baltimore welcomes about 11 million visitors.

THE FUTURE

Like Baltimore, Chesapeake Bay is a vital resource for Maryland's people and its economy. In the 1960s, private citizens and the governments of the states surrounding the bay began to take action to improve the health of the bay. Then, in the 1970s, Maryland senator Charles Matthias got the U.S. Congress interested, and the public at large began to care.

When Baltimore mayor Martin O'Malley was sworn in as Maryland's governor in January 2007, he told Marylanders to make the commitment to "rescuing this natural jewel—of fusing science, government and personal responsibility" to preserving the state's quality of life and Chesapeake Bay.

Part of the state's plan for moving forward was passage of the nation's first "living wage" law. This law, signed and put into effect in 2007, requires companies receiving state contracts to pay well above the national minimum wage. The legislators believe that government has an important role in fighting poverty.

Governor O'Malley also reviewed Maryland's history and signed a formal apology for slavery. Maryland was the second state (after neighboring Virginia) to offer African Americans such an apology.

Annapolis and the Chesapeake Bay

READ ABOUT

Marylanders enjoying a beach day at Ocean City.

Wh...
Mar...

The colors
throughout
people live

People pe...
- 1,...
- 2...
- 5(...
- 1(...
- 1(...

accent t...
foreign ...
their sp...
dialect ...
employ ...
would u...

CHAPTER SIX

PEOPLE

★

IF YOU LIVE IN MARYLAND, THE BIG CITY NEAREST YOU IS PROBABLY BALTIMORE OR WASHINGTON, D.C. At least four-fifths of Maryland's people live within 40 miles (64 km) of those cities, which are only 38 miles (61 km) apart. Together, they make up the fourth-largest metropolitan area in the country. Only New York, Los Angeles, and Chicago are larger.

How does Maryland compare to other states in total population? In 2006, Maryland was the 19th most populous state, home to 1.85 percent of the nation's people.

Maryland is famous for its seafood.

Students and their
terrapin to the wild
Maryland.

WOW

The biggest crab cake of all was
made in 2006 by an Eastern
Shore company. It served
800 people and weighed 225
pounds (102 kg), a Guinness
World Record.

Big Cit

This list shows the
Maryland's bigges

Baltimore . . . . .
Rockville . . . .
Frederick . . . .
Gaithersburg . .
Bowie . . . .

Source: U.S. Census Bureau

HOW TO TALK LIKE
A MARYLANDER

People who lived on Maryland's Eastern Shore were
long isolated from the rest of the state. They developed
some words for things that are different from those on
the Western Shore. For example, on Tangier Island, a
praying mantis is called a horse hopper. Sailors know
that "airish" means "cold and windy." Some other
Eastern Shore terms are "like to" for "almost"; "own
cousin" for "first cousin"; and "carry," meaning to go
with someone to a function.

HOW TO EAT LIKE
A MARYLANDER

The state of Maryland is famous for its blue crabs, and
all kinds of seafood are popular. But Marylanders also
enjoy fresh produce, such as apples, potatoes, tomatoes, corn, and sweet potatoes from local farms. Fried
chicken is a favorite for many Marylanders, too.

MENU

WHAT'S ON THE MENU IN MARYLAND?

★ ★ ★

Apples

Maryland's apple orchards produce countless varieties, including Empire, Fuji, York, Gala, Ginger Gold, and McIntosh. They're delicious baked into pies and muffins, made into apple sauce or cider, or fresh off the tree.

Fried Tomatoes

Tomatoes are sliced and dipped in bread crumbs, then sautéed for a crispy treat.

Blue Crabs

What's the best way to eat blue crabs? Any way you can is one answer. You can have them steamed, fried, or barbequed. But the best way to enjoy a Maryland crab feast is sitting with friends around a plastic-cloth-covered table piled high with freshly steamed whole crabs. Crack the shells open, pick out the meat, and enjoy every succulent morsel.

TRY THIS RECIPE
Maryland Crab Cakes

Maryland is famous for its blue crabs. One of the most delicious ways to enjoy them is in crab cakes. You can find fresh crabmeat at a fish market or canned crab at the grocery store. The bigger the chunks of crab, the better the crab cakes. Be sure to remove any bits of shell or cartilage that might be in the meat.

Ingredients:
1 cup Italian-style seasoned bread crumbs
1 large egg, lightly beaten
¼ cup mayonnaise
1 teaspoon mustard powder
1 teaspoon Worcestershire sauce
½ teaspoon seafood seasoning (optional)
½ teaspoon salt
¼ teaspoon pepper
1 pound crabmeat
Butter or oil
Tartar sauce

Instructions:
Combine the first eight ingredients in a bowl and mix thoroughly. Gently fold in the crabmeat, and try to keep the chunks from breaking up. Refrigerate the mixture for an hour. With clean hands, shape the chilled mixture into 6 patties. Heat a little butter or oil in a frying pan over medium heat. Cook the crab cakes until browned, about 5 minutes on each side. Serve with tartar sauce, and eat like a Marylander.

Crab cakes

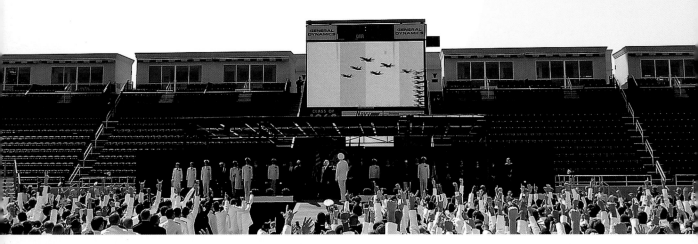

The U.S. Navy's Blue Angels perform a flyover during graduation at the U.S. Naval Academy in Annapolis.

EDUCATION

In colonial times, schooling was mainly for boys, and they were taught by local ministers or sent back to England for school. Today, all children between 5 and 16 years old are required to attend school, unless they are homeschooled.

In 1845, Congress voted to establish a naval academy at Annapolis. Over the next 50 years, the U.S. Naval Academy grew in size and stature. Today, to be accepted in the four-year program, most students have to be recommended by their senator or representative in Congress. The academy has a student body of about 4,000.

Marylanders are proud of their excellent system of higher education. St. John's College in Annapolis opened in 1784. Its unique curriculum focuses on the classics.

The school that became the University of Maryland was chartered in 1856 as Maryland Agricultural College. In 1954, it became the first state university in the South with both black and white students. Today, the university system combines 11 different colleges and campuses. The main campus is in College Park.

Johns Hopkins University was founded in 1876 as a research institution. Its hospital was founded in 1889, and four years later became a medical school. It is one of the leading medical research centers in the world.

WRITERS AND ARTISTS

Maryland has produced plenty of wonderful writers. One of the earliest was Benjamin Banneker. A mathematician and astronomer, he published the first of his almanacs in 1792. The Banneker-Douglass Museum in Annapolis honors both Benjamin Banneker and writer Frederick Douglass.

Poet and humorist Ogden Nash (1902–1971) lived in Baltimore. He was best known for his silly ways with words, such as in this helpful rhyme:

The one-L lama, he's a priest
The two-L llama, he's a beast

Children's book author Munro Leaf created the ever-popular story about a bull, *The Story of Ferdinand.* He

ABOLITIONIST AND NOVELIST

Frances Ellen Watkins Harper (1825–1911) was born in Baltimore to free black parents. She began writing poetry when she was a teenager. Her poems were published in abolitionist magazines and in a volume called *Autumn Leaves.* She later taught at colleges and worked on the Underground Railroad. She became even more active in the cause of abolition when she was kept from returning to Maryland by a law that allowed free blacks to be sold into slavery. In 1892, her novel Iola *Leroy, or Shadows Uplifted* was published. It's about a wealthy slave owner who falls in love with and marries an African American woman. It is believed to be the first novel published by an African American woman in the United States.

CHARLES WILLSON PEALE: MARYLAND'S FAMILY OF ARTISTS

Marylanders and other early Americans were happy to sit still for a portrait by painter Charles Willson Peale (1741–1827). A native of Queen Anne's County, Peale lived in Annapolis but traveled widely to paint portraits of the leaders of the various colonies. He also painted now-famous pictures of events during the American Revolution. Peale was the father of 17 children, all of whom became artists. He was also interested in natural history and inventions, and in 1784 he and his friends created the Peale Museum, which is managed by the Maryland Historical Society.

? Want to know more? www.msa.md.gov/msa/speccol/1545/html/1032.html

lived in Garrett Park. Priscilla Cummings of Annapolis is the author of a popular series of children's books featuring a Chesapeake blue crab named Chadwick.

Poet, short-story writer, and critic Edgar Allan Poe moved to Baltimore in 1829 to live with a widowed aunt. In Baltimore, he wrote a number of short stories. He died in the city in 1849 at the age of 40.

ENTERTAINERS

Ragtime is one of America's great contributions to popular music, and the best-known name in ragtime is Eubie Blake. Born in Baltimore to former slaves, Blake got his start playing the piano for tips in saloons. But in 1921, he and his friend Noble Sissle wrote the musical *Shuffle Along*—the first Broadway play ever produced that was written and directed by African Americans. A musical based on Blake's work, called *Eubie,* was produced on Broadway in 1978.

The great jazz singer Billie Holiday (named Eleanora Fagan by her parents) grew up in Baltimore. Frank Zappa, another Baltimorean, was one of the big names of rock music in the 1960s and 1970s. Tori Amos, pop singer and composer, was raised in Baltimore and Rockville. Her first single, recorded in 1980, was called "Baltimore."

Baltimore-raised Tori Amos performs at the Hammersmith Apollo in London.

Jim Henson, the creator of the Muppets, was born in Mississippi but spent his teen years in Hyattsville. He started making puppets for TV, and while a student at the University of Maryland, had a regular show called *Sam and Friends*. One "friend" was an early version of Kermit the Frog. In 1968, he was asked to create segments for *Sesame Street*. He introduced Cookie Monster, Big Bird, and their friends to the world.

FAQ

Q8 WHAT DID OPRAH WINFREY DO IN MARYLAND?

A8 The world-famous talk show host was working in Nashville, Tennessee, when she was hired by a Baltimore TV station to read the news. Oprah didn't like reading what someone else had written, so the TV station gave her a chance to host a daytime talk show called *People Are Talking*. Her work in Baltimore daytime television from 1977 to 1983 brought her to the attention of a much bigger station in Chicago. The rest is history!

Orioles Park at Camden Yards is a fan favorite.

A Thoroughbred named Man O' War trained at Glen Riddle Farm in Berlin, Maryland. He is often considered the greatest American racehorse ever.

SPORTS

The city of Baltimore recognized its namesake bird by naming its hometown baseball team the Baltimore Orioles in the 1880s. The original Baltimore Orioles won their first professional baseball championship in 1894, the first of three National League pennants. But that team was disbanded in 1899. In 1954, after decades in the minor leagues, the newer Orioles were accepted into major league baseball. They won their first World Series in 1966 and again in 1970 and in 1983. In 1992, the team moved to a new stadium in downtown Baltimore, Orioles Park at Camden Yards.

The Maryland Jockey Club is the oldest sporting organization in the United States. It is headquartered at Baltimore's Pimlico Race Course, which opened in 1870. Pimlico is home to the Preakness Stakes, the second race of the famous Triple Crown in Thoroughbred horse racing. (The first race is the Kentucky Derby in Louisville, Kentucky, and the third is the Belmont Stakes in New York.) If a horse wins all three races in one season, it is known as a Triple Crown winner.

It was Maryland's history of horse racing that gave Baltimore's football team its name, the Colts. The Colts played in Maryland starting in 1947, but the team didn't receive much attention until Johnny Unitas ("The Golden Arm"), son of a Lithuanian immigrant family from East Baltimore, became the Colts quarterback in 1956. The Baltimore Colts became the Indianapolis Colts in 1984, leaving Maryland in the middle of the night and stunning their fans with the move.

But professional football was far from over in Maryland. The Cleveland Browns moved up to Baltimore in 1996, becoming the Ravens, and found their way to a Super Bowl championship in 2001. The team mascots are three ravens—named Edgar, Allan, and Poe.

MINI-BIO

BABE RUTH: THE SULTAN OF SWAT

Babe Ruth (1895–1948) was born George Herman Ruth in Baltimore. In 1914, he joined the minor league Baltimore Orioles as a left-handed pitcher. The scout who discovered him called him his "babe," giving him the nickname. The major league Boston Red Sox took him on, and he pitched in his first World Series game at age 21. The New York Yankees bought his contract for a then-record amount because of his incredible ability at bat, which gave Ruth his other nickname, The Sultan of Swat. In 1927, he hit 60 home runs, a record not matched until 1961 when Roger Maris hit 61. Ruth was one of the first five players inducted into the Baseball Hall of Fame. Babe's birthplace in Baltimore is now a museum.

? **Want to know more?** See www.baberuth.com/

Maryland's own Cal Ripken Jr. played his entire career for the Baltimore Orioles. He was elected to the Baseball Hall of Fame in 2007. Called the Iron Man, he played a phenomenal 2,632 consecutive games and is considered one of the best shortstops of all time.

READ ABOUT

The Maryland House of Delegates holds an opening session at the statehouse.

CHAPTER SEVEN

GOVERNMENT

★

Maryland has had four constitutions in its history. The first was written in 1776, when the colonies were breaking away from Britain. It called for a government "of the people" and didn't mention the king. A second state constitution was adopted in 1851. It made Baltimore City into a government body equal to a county. The rest of the document concerned the courts. A third constitution, written in 1864, abolished slavery as of November 1 of that year. The constitution in effect today was written in 1867, though it has been amended many times since then.

Annapolis was capital of the new United States for a few months. The Continental Congress met in Maryland's statehouse from November 26, 1783, to June 3, 1784. It was there that the Treaty of Paris was ratified, ending the American Revolution.

THE CAPITAL AND THE CAPITOL

Where Annapolis sits today on the Severn River, there was once a settlement called Providence. It was founded in 1649 by Puritans from Virginia, who no longer felt welcome there. When the capital was moved there in 1694, the name was changed to Annapolis, for Princess Anne, queen of Great Britain and Ireland in 1702. Annapolis is also home to the U.S. Naval Academy.

The original capitol, or statehouse, in St. Mary's City, was built in 1676 by Captain John Quigley. Archaeologists found the site of the original statehouse, and in 1934 it was reconstructed to celebrate Maryland's 300th anniversary. It is now part of Historic St. Mary's City, a National Historic Landmark.

Maryland's Capital

This map shows places of interest in Annapolis, Maryland's capital city.

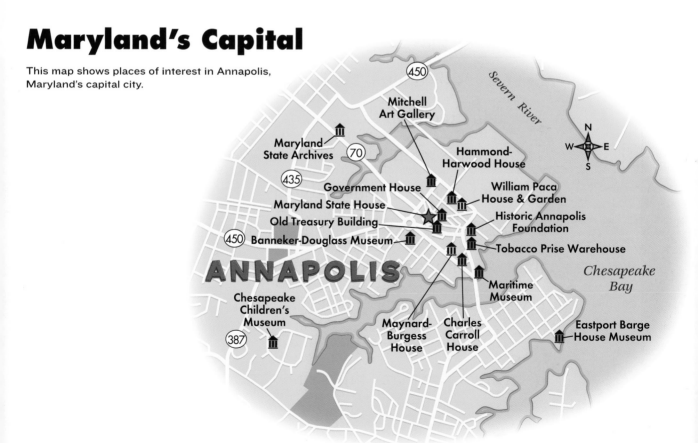

Meanwhile, in Annapolis, the first capitol burned, and the second one was considered so ugly that the assembly decided to have it torn down. The capitol that stands today was built in 1772 on the same site. It is the oldest capitol in the country still in use by a state's legislature. Its dome, the oldest and largest wooden dome in the United States, is topped by a wooden acorn that supports a lightning rod designed by Benjamin Franklin.

The Maryland State House in Annapolis

Capitol Facts

Here are some interesting facts about Maryland's state capitol.

Height: 181 feet (55 m) to weather vane
Dome interior height: 113 feet (34 m)
Dome diameter at base: 40 feet (12 m)
Size of acorn: 5 feet (1.5 m) tall. The acorn, which provides stability for Franklin's lightning rod, was replaced in 1996 because the original had rotted.
Lightning rod: 28 feet (8.5 m) tall

WEIRD AND WACKY LAWS

- In Baltimore, it's against the law to take a lion to the movies.
- If you go jogging in a public park, you must wear a shirt with sleeves.
- In Columbia, you cannot hang clothes on a line in the backyard. You can, however, drape them over a fence.
- Ocean City laws say that you may not eat while swimming.

approved by the Senate for terms of 10 years. If they want to continue in office, Marylanders have to approve them by vote. The Court of Appeals also reviews legislation to be sure it's in line with the state's constitution. A Court of Special Appeals was created to ease some of the workload from the Court of Appeals.

Maryland Counties

This map shows the 23 counties plus Baltimore City in Maryland. Annapolis, the state capital, is indicated with a star.

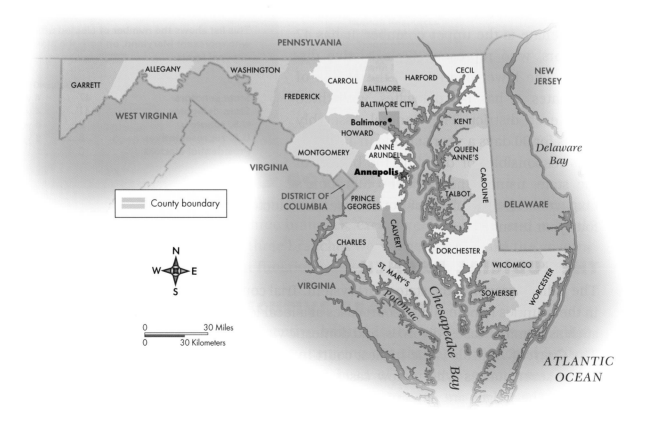

DIVISIONS OF THE STATE

Maryland is arranged in 24 divisions—23 counties plus Baltimore City (there is also a Baltimore County). Kent, on the northeastern shore, is the smallest county. Frederick, in the Piedmont, is the largest. Kent County has the smallest population (19,899 people in 2005), while Montgomery, on the north side of Washington, D.C., has the largest (927,583 people).

Maryland's county governments wield a lot of power. Even some of the biggest towns, such as Columbia, do not have their own government. Instead, they are run by their county. When asked where they live, Marylanders are more likely to name their county than their town.

Baltimore mayor Martin O'Malley (right) shakes hands with a member of the Baltimore Youth Congress in 2004. O'Malley became governor of Maryland in 2007.

An engineer works on a camera for the Hubble Space Telescope at Maryland's NASA Goddard Space Flight Center.

THE FEDERAL FACTOR

Several important federal agencies and military facilities are located in Maryland. These include Camp Meade, now Fort Meade, which was established by the federal government in 1917. That same year, the U.S. Army established Aberdeen Proving Ground on Chesapeake Bay. The National Institutes of Health is in Bethesda. NASA's Goddard Space Flight Center is in Greenbelt, the U.S. Census Bureau is in Prince Georges County, the Social Security Administration is in Baltimore County, and the National Security Agency is located on the grounds of Fort Meade. The National Oceanographic and Atmospheric Administration, which includes the U.S. Weather Bureau, is in Rockville.

Parren Mitchell of Baltimore was Maryland's first African American congressman. He was elected in 1970 and served until 1987. The first woman to serve in the U.S. House of Representatives from Maryland was Katharine Edgar Byron from Williamsport, elected in 1941. She was elected following the death of her congressman husband. Barbara Mikulski, the first Maryland woman elected to the U.S. Senate, took office in 1987.

Maryland's U.S. senators Ben Cardin and Barbara Mikulski in 2006

MINI-BIO

NANCY PELOSI: MADAME SPEAKER

In January 2007, for the first time in U.S. history, a woman was directly in line to become president of the United States. Baltimore native Nancy Pelosi was elected Speaker of the U.S. House of Representatives. The Speaker is second in line, behind the vice president, to become president if the president is unable to serve a complete term. Pelosi, a Democrat from San Francisco, California, was born Nancy D'Alesandro in Baltimore in 1940. Her father was a congressman and served as mayor of Baltimore, as did her brother. Referring to the challenges women face in rising to top positions in industry and government, Pelosi said, "The marble ceiling has been broken!"

? Want to know more? See http://speaker.house. gov/about/

State Flag

Maryland's flag is divided into quarters. The upper left and lower right quarters show the black and gold coat of arms of the first Lord Baltimore, George Calvert. These are the state's official colors. The other two quarters feature the red and white cross of the coat of arms of the Crosslands, Calvert's mother's family.

The design for the flag was taken from the state seal, which shows the Calvert and Crossland coats of arms on a shield. Flags with this design were first flown in the late 19th century, and in 1904 the current flag was officially adopted as the state flag.

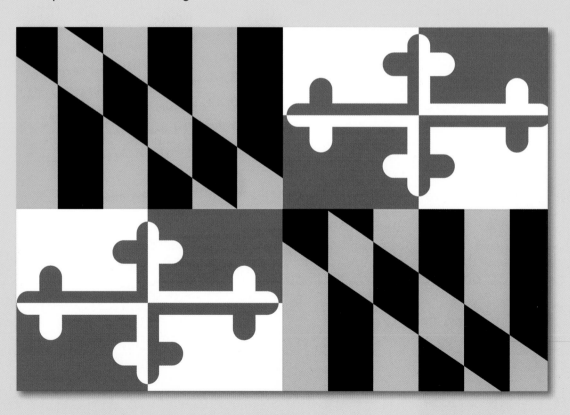

State Seal

The reverse of the Great Seal of Maryland consists of a shield bearing the Calvert and Crossland coats of arms quartered. Above is an earl's coronet and a full-faced helmet. The shield is supported on one side by a farmer and on the other by a fisherman. It symbolizes Lord Baltimore's two estates: Maryland and Avalon in Newfoundland.

The obverse of the Great Seal of Maryland shows Lord Baltimore as a knight in full armor mounted on a charger. The inscription translated is "Cecilius, Absolute Lord of Maryland and Avalon, Baron of Baltimore."

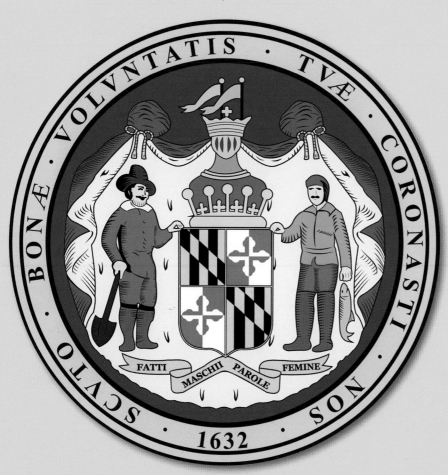

98

Service workers, such as this firefighter, form a large part of Maryland's economy.

CHAPTER EIGHT

ECONOMY

★

MARYLAND IS THE WEALTHIEST STATE IN THE UNITED STATES. But while many residents hold high-paying professional jobs, other people struggle to make ends meet. As the Maryland economy shifts from one based on manufacturing, agriculture, and fishing to one based on service and technology industries, the need for a diverse and skilled workforce will continue to grow.

THE SERVICE INDUSTRY

While Maryland's economy still relies on the manufacturing of goods and the production of food, most people work in the service industry. This part of the workforce includes teachers and doctors, salespeople, government employees, lawyers, social workers, bankers, chefs, and computer programmers.

Many of Maryland's service employees actually work outside the state, in Washington, D.C. They commute to the city to work for the military and federal agencies.

Schools throughout Maryland employ professors and many administrative workers. Hospitals provide jobs for nurses, surgeons, and many other medical professionals.

BIG BUSINESS

Alonzo G. Decker and S. Duncan Black had a small machine shop in Baltimore, which manufactured an electric drill designed by Decker. A few years later, they were awarded a patent on the drill's pistol grip. Today, Black & Decker is the world's largest manufacturer of power tools. Its headquarters is in Towson.

WOW

Dairyman Jacob Fussell opened America's first ice cream factory in Baltimore in 1851.

A Silver Spring English teacher answers a student's question.

A research scientist at work in a Rockville biotechnology lab.

Next time you reach for the cinnamon for your toast, check the label. McCormick and Company is headquartered in Baltimore. Founded in 1889, the company made flavorings and syrups. Later, the firm bought a spice company. McCormick is now one of the world's largest harvesters and sellers of quality spices.

Maryland is home to a number of leading companies and institutions in the field of **biotechnology**. Developments in this field can be used in health and medicine, the environment, and agriculture, to name just a few. Biotechnology is one of the modern industries that has replaced steelmaking and shipbuilding to help bring Maryland's economy into the 21st century.

WORD TO KNOW

biotechnology *the manipulation of living organisms for developments in the areas of food production, waste disposal, mining, and medicine*

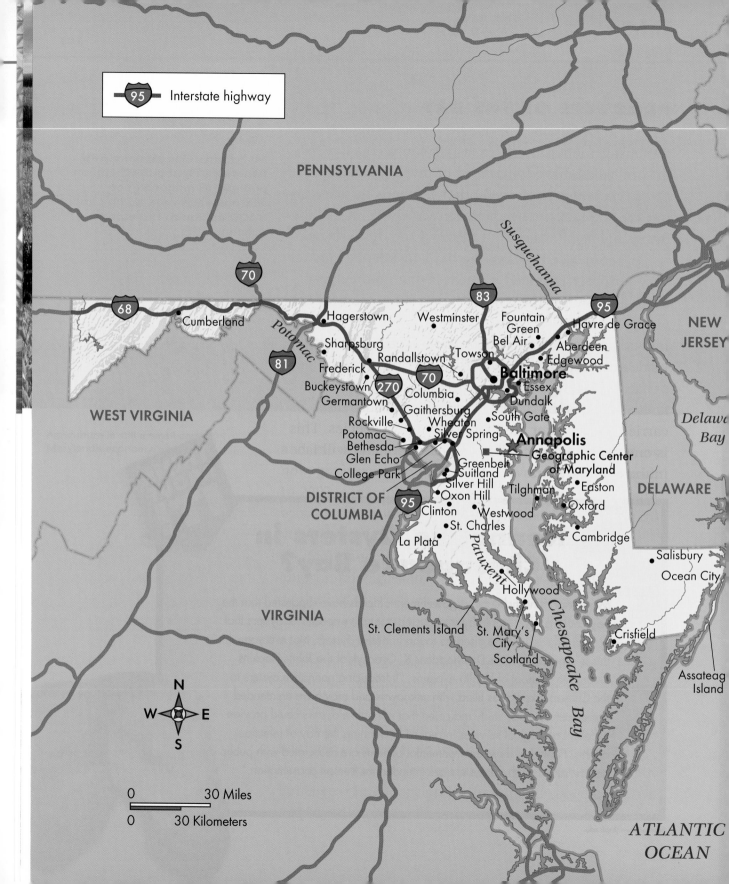

PENNSYLVANIA

Susquehanna

Interstate highway
95

70
68

Cumberland

81

Potomac

WEST VIRGINIA

Hagerstown
Westminster
Fountain
Green
Havre de Grace
83
95
Sharpsburg
Bel Air
Aberdeen
Randallstown
Towson
Edgewood
Frederick
70
Baltimore
Buckeystown
270
Columbia
Essex
Germantown
Dundalk
Gaithersburg
Rockville
Wheaton
South Gate
Potomac
Silver Spring
Annapolis
Bethesda
Glen Echo
Greenbelt
★ **Geographic Center**
of Maryland
College Park
Suitland
Silver Hill
Tilghman
Easton
DISTRICT OF
Oxon Hill
Oxford
COLUMBIA
95
Clinton
Westwood
St. Charles
Cambridge
La Plata

VIRGINIA

Patuxent

Salisbury
Ocean City

Hollywood

St. Clements Island
St. Mary's
City
Scotland

Crisfield

Chesapeake Bay

NEW
JERSEY

Delaware
Bay

DELAWARE

Assateag
Island

N
W E
S

0   30 Miles
0   30 Kilometers

ATLANTIC
OCEAN

CHAPTER NINE

TRAVEL GUIDE

★

THERE'S A GOOD REASON WHY MARY-LAND HAS OFTEN BEEN CALLED "AMERICA IN MINIATURE." It has mountains, beaches, big cities, small towns, farms, and thriving industry. And when you come to visit, you'll want to see it all. So grab your map and follow along as we take a trip through the Old Line State.

← Follow along with this travel map. We'll begin in Baltimore and travel all the way down to Ocean City!

BALTIMORE

THINGS TO DO: Visit historic sites that played a role in shaping the nation, or explore the USS *Constellation* at the historic seaport.

Baltimore's Inner Harbor

Baltimore

★ **Monuments:** In the heart of the city is the Battle Monument, which honors those who died protecting the city during the Battle of Baltimore. It so impressed President John Quincy Adams that he called Baltimore "Monument City." Built in 1829, the Washington Monument was the first to commemorate President George Washington.

★ **Fort McHenry:** This star-shaped fort sits on a peninsula that juts into Baltimore Harbor. After helping protect the new United States in 1814, it served as a prison during the Civil War. It's a great place to observe Maryland's Defenders Day on September 12, when you can still see the rockets' red glare!

★ **The Inner Harbor:** What's the most popular tourist attraction in Maryland? It's the National Aquarium at the Inner Harbor. Here you can see more than 16,500 creatures! Be sure to visit the observation deck atop Baltimore's World Trade Center for a great view of the harbor, the city, and beyond. It is the world's tallest five-sided (pentagonal) building.

★ **The Seaport:** Baltimore's seaport has been active for almost 300 years. In the late 1970s, it was completely rebuilt and renovated. In the harbor you'll see historic ships, such as the USS *Constellation*, the last sailing ship built for the U.S. Navy during the Civil War. The Baltimore Maritime Museum has a World War II submarine, the *Torsk*, as well as other historic ships.

Fort McHenry

★ **Camden Yards:** Opened in 1992, this stadium, home field of baseball's Baltimore Orioles, is officially called Oriole Park at Camden Yards. In 2005, the Sports Legends Museum was opened at Camden Yards. It is operated by the Babe Ruth Museum and houses memorabilia of the Orioles, Ravens, and Maryland sports.

★ **Pimlico Race Course:** This is the place to be on the third Saturday in May. That's when the Preakness Stakes is run. It's the second of three horse races that make up the world-famous Triple Crown.

Pimlico Race Course

GATEWAY TO THE NATION'S CAPITAL

THINGS TO DO: Heading toward Washington, D.C., stop in Annapolis and explore the U.S. Naval Academy or visit the Banneker-Douglass Museum, which preserves the history of African Americans in Maryland.

Annapolis

★ **U.S. Naval Academy:** Explore the U.S. Naval Academy where John Paul Jones, founder of the U.S. Navy, is buried and where midshipmen learn the ways of the seas.

★ **Banneker-Douglass Museum:** Named for Benjamin Banneker and Frederick Douglass, this museum preserves Maryland's African American heritage and is the state's official museum for the preservation of African American material.

★ **Maryland State House:** The capitol in Annapolis is the oldest state capitol still in use. A must-see!

Replica of *Maryland Federalist* in Maryland State House

ALEX HALEY AND HIS SLAVE ANCESTOR

An enslaved African named Kunta Kinte arrived in Annapolis, probably in 1767. He was an ancestor of writer Alex Haley (1921–1992), who in 1976 published a book called *Roots*, which traced his family's history back to Kunta Kinte. The book was later made into a popular TV miniseries. A Kunta Kinte Heritage Festival is held annually at the Anne Arundel County Fairgrounds in Crownsville. There's a statue dedicated to Haley in Annapolis.

Glen Echo

★ **Clara Barton National Historic Site:** Called the "Angel of the Battlefield," Clara Barton nursed soldiers on both sides during the Civil War, and she devoted her life to serving others. Her home was used as headquarters, a warehouse, and living space for the American Red Cross, an organization she founded.

★ **Glen Echo Park:** This facility near Clara Barton's home was a popular amusement park from 1898 to 1968, and it has since become an arts and education center. Children of all ages are drawn to the Dentzel Carousel, which dates from 1921. Visitors can enjoy a picnic area, watch puppet shows, and take part in a dance program at the Spanish Ballroom.

College Park

★ **College Park Airport and Aviation Museum:** The College Park Airport is the world's oldest continuously operating airport and was founded in 1909 when Wilbur Wright came to instruct World War I aviators. The museum highlights the many "firsts" that occurred at the airport.

SEE IT HERE!

"CHARGE, SIR KNIGHT!"

Would you like to get a glimpse of what it was like to be a knight during the Middle Ages? The oldest jousting competition in the United States was founded in 1950 by the Maryland Jousting Tournament Association. In 1962, it was named the State Sport of Maryland. You can see jousting in action throughout Maryland, but especially at the Renaissance Festival, held in the autumn at Crownsville.

Maryland's Renaissance Festival

Greenbelt

★ **Goddard Space Flight Center:** Goddard was the first National Aeronautics and Space Administration (NASA) center to explore space, and it's still one of the most important. Its satellites provide data on Earth and the environment, and its large space-borne telescopes keep an eye on the universe.

BETWEEN TWO RIVERS

THINGS TO DO: Explore the two great Western Shore rivers, visit the site of Maryland's original capital, or tour the Potomac River Museum and see murals of Maryland's history.

St. Mary's City

★ **Historic St. Mary's City:** The original capital of the Maryland Colony, the site is now a living history museum, featuring reconstructions of the original statehouse and many private homes.

The Calvert penny as seen at St. Mary's City

St. Clement's Island

St. Clements Island

★ **St. Clements Island State Park:** This is where the first European colonists' ships, the *Ark* and the *Dove*, landed on March 25, 1634. Don't miss the Potomac River Museum with its murals of Maryland history.

Hollywood

★ **Sotterley Plantation:** A plantation has stood on the Patuxent River for more than 300 years. The great plantation house served as an inspiration to George Washington when he was planning his home, Mount Vernon.

Scotland

★ **Point Lookout State Park:** This park is the southernmost point of Maryland, jutting into the bay where it meets the Potomac River. Originally owned by Governor Leonard Calvert, it became an infamous prisoner-of-war camp during the Civil War.

INTO THE MOUNTAINS

THINGS TO DO: Explore a Civil War battlefield, ride the Western Maryland Scenic Railway, or hike the Appalachian Trail.

Sharpsburg

★ **Antietam National Battlefield:** Explore the site of the bloodiest battle of the Civil War. Nearby in Frederick is the Monocacy National Battlefield, also worthy of a visit.

Cumberland

★ **Cumberland:** The largest city in western Maryland lies in a valley, overlooking a natural pass, or opening, in the mountains. It was because of this pass that the Cumberland Road (later called the National Road) to the Ohio River began here. You'll see where George Washington started his military career.

Buckeystown

★ **Water Lilies:** A great place for a picnic, Lilypons Water Gardens near Buckeystown features acres of water lily and goldfish ponds. Founded in 1917, the 300-acre (121-ha) garden was named to honor operatic soprano Lily Pons.

Hagerstown

★ **Alsatia Mummers Parade Festival:** For almost 100 years, Hagerstown has hosted this annual Halloween parade, held at night. Nearly 10,000 people participate in various activities. Alsatia is the name of a club in Hagerstown, and Mummers are people in costumes and masks.

THE EASTERN SHORE

THINGS TO DO: Visit historic sites, swim in the ocean, sail on the bay, or go crabbing.

Crisfield

★ **J. Millard Tawes Historical Museum:** Here, you'll see how early Marylanders lived.

Tilghman

★ **The *Rebecca T. Ruark*:** Take a trip on the *Rebecca T. Ruark*. Built in 1886, it is the oldest working skipjack on Chesapeake Bay.

The wild ponies on Assateague

Assateague Island

★ **Assateague Island National Seashore:** Assateague and Ocean City were once connected, but a 1933 hurricane rearranged things. The large Chincoteague Bay is protected by Assateague Island. Here you'll find the world-famous wild ponies, and you can explore life on a barrier island.

Ocean City

★ **Ocean City Boardwalk:** Ocean City stretches along the narrow barrier island, with the ocean to the east and Isle of Wight Bay and Sinepuxent Bay to the west. This is the state's only seacoast, and it's a place of sandy beaches and a world-famous, 3-mile-long (4.8 km) boardwalk!

The *Rebecca T. Ruark*

WRITING PROJECTS

★ ★ ★

Create an Election Brochure or Web Site!
Run for office!
Throughout this book, you've read about some of the issues that concern Maryland today.

★ As a candidate for governor of Maryland, create a campaign brochure or Web site.

★ Explain how you meet the qualifications to be governor of Maryland, and talk about the three or four major issues you'll focus on if you're elected.

★ Remember, you'll be responsible for Maryland's budget. How would you spend the taxpayers' money?

SEE: Chapter Seven, pages 86–95.

GO TO: Maryland's government Web site at www.maryland.gov

Compare and Contrast— When, Why, and How Did They Come?
Compare the migration and explorations of the Native people and the first European explorers. Tell about:

★ When their migrations began

★ How they traveled

★ Why they migrated

★ Where their journeys began and ended

★ What they found when they arrived

SEE: Chapters Two and Three, pages 26–33 and 34–47.

Write a Memoir, Journal, or Editorial for Your School Newspaper!
Picture Yourself . . .

★ attending the Continental Congress. Talk to the other people who are attending. What ideas would you have for the new nation?

SEE: Chapter Three, pages 45–46.

★ attending a political conference at Camp David. Think about the leaders who would be there. What issues would you discuss?

SEE: Chapter Five, page 69.

President Jimmy Carter (center) meets with Egyptian president Anwar Sadat (left) and Israeli prime minister Menachem Begin (right) at Camp David in 1978.

ART PROJECTS

★ ★ ★

Create a PowerPoint Presentation or Visitors' Guide

Welcome to Maryland!

Maryland's a great place to visit and to live. From its natural beauty to its bustling cities and historic sites, there's plenty to see and do. In your PowerPoint presentation or brochure, highlight 10 to 15 of Maryland's amazing landmarks. Be sure to include:

★ a map of the state showing where these sites are located

★ photos, illustrations, Web links, natural history facts, geographic stats, climate and weather, plants and wildlife, recent discoveries.

SEE: Chapter Nine, pages 108–115.

GO TO: The official Web site of Maryland tourism at www.mdisfun.org. Download and print maps, photos, national landmark images, and vacation ideas for tourists.

Illustrate the Lyrics to the Maryland State Song

("Maryland, My Maryland")

Use markers, paints, photos, collage, colored pencils, or computer graphics to illustrate the lyrics to "Maryland, My Maryland," the state song. Turn your illustrations into a picture book, or scan them into a PowerPoint and add music!

SEE: The lyrics to "Maryland, My Maryland" on page 128.

GO TO: The Maryland state Web site at www. maryland.gov to find out more about the origin of the Maryland state song, "Maryland, My Maryland."

State Quarter Project

From 1999 to 2008, the U.S. Mint introduced new quarters commemorating each of the 50 states in the order that they were admitted into the Union. Each state's quarter features a unique design on its reverse, or back.

★ Research and write an essay explaining:

the significance of each image

who designed the quarter

who chose the final design

★ Design your own Maryland quarter. What images would you choose for the reverse?

★ Make a poster showing the Maryland quarter and label each image.

GO TO: www.usmint.gov/kids and find out what's featured on the back of the Maryland quarter.

SCIENCE, TECHNOLOGY, & MATH PROJECTS

★ ★ ★

Graph Population Statistics

★ Compare population statistics (such as ethnic background, birth, death, and literacy rates) in Maryland counties or major cities.

★ In your graph or chart, look at population density, and write sentences describing what the population statistics show; graph one set of population statistics, and write a paragraph explaining what the graphs reveal.

SEE: Chapter Six, pages 74–77.

GO TO: The official Web site for the U.S. Census Bureau at www.census.gov, and at http://quickfacts.census.gov/qfd/states/24000.html to find out more about population statistics, how they work, and what the statistics are for Maryland.

Create a Weather Map of Maryland

Use your knowledge of Maryland's geography to research and identify conditions that result in specific weather events. Create a weather map or poster that shows the weather patterns over the state. To accompany your map, explain the technology used to measure weather phenomena.

SEE: Chapter One, pages 24–25.

GO TO: The National Oceanic and Atmospheric Administration's National Weather Service Web site at www.weather.gov for weather maps and forecasts for Maryland.

Track Endangered Species

Using your knowledge of Maryland's wildlife, research what animals and plants are endangered or threatened. Find out what the state is doing to protect these species. Chart known populations of the animals and plants, and report on changes in certain geographical areas.

SEE: Chapter One, page 20.

GO TO: The U.S. Fish and Wildlife site at www.endangeredspecie.com/states/md.htm or other Maryland-specific sites.

Delmarva fox squirrel

PRIMARY VS. SECONDARY SOURCES

★ ★ ★

What's the Diff?

Your teacher may require at least one or two primary sources and one or two secondary sources for your assignment. So, what's the difference between the two?

★ **Primary sources are original.** You are reading the actual words of someone's diary, journal, letter, autobiography, or interview. Primary sources can also be photographs, maps, prints, cartoons, news/film footage, posters, first-person newspaper articles, drawings, musical scores, and recordings. By the way, when you conduct a survey, interview someone, make a video, or take photographs to include in a project, you are creating primary sources.

★ **Secondary sources are what you find in encyclopedias, textbooks, articles, biographies, and almanacs.** These are written by a person or group of people who tell about something that happened to someone else. Secondary sources also recount what another person said or did. This book is an example of a secondary source.

Now that you know what primary sources are—where can you find them?

★ **Your school or local library:** Check the library catalog for collections of original writings, government documents, musical scores, and so on. Some of this material may be stored on microfilm. The Library of Congress Web site (www.loc.gov) is an excellent online resource for primary source materials.

★ **Historical societies:** These organizations keep historical documents, photographs, and other materials. Staff members can help you find what you are looking for. History museums are also great places to see primary sources firsthand.

★ **The Internet:** There are lots of sites that have primary sources you can download and use in a project or assignment.

Letters issued to explorer John Cabot

TIMELINE

★ ★ ★

U.S. Events `1400` **Maryland Events**

1492
Christopher Columbus and his crew sight land in the Caribbean Sea.

1498
Britain claims the land around the Chesapeake Bay based on sightings by explorer John Cabot.

`1500`

1565
Spanish admiral Pedro Menéndez de Avilés founds St. Augustine, Florida, the oldest continuously occupied European settlement in the continental United States.

1572
Spanish explorer Pedro Menéndez de Avilés enters Chesapeake Bay.

1587
The entrance to Chesapeake Bay first appears on a map.

`1600`

1607
The first permanent English settlement is established in North America at Jamestown.

1608
Captain John Smith of Virginia explores Chesapeake Bay.

1619
The first African indentured laborers in English North America are purchased for work in the Jamestown settlement.

1630
The Beaver Wars begin.

1634
The first colonists arrive aboard the *Ark* and the *Dove*.

1642
African Mathias de Sousa is elected to the assembly.

Mathias de Sousa

1664
First law enslaving all black people is passed by the assembly.

1682
René-Robert Cavelier, Sieur de La Salle, claims more than 1 million square miles (2.6 million sq km) of territory in the Mississippi River basin for France, naming it Louisiana.

1694
The capital is moved to Annapolis.

U.S. Events — 1700 — Maryland Events

1729
Baltimore is founded.

1776
Thirteen American colonies declare their independence from Great Britain.

1783
November 26, Annapolis begins to serve as the capital of the new nation.

1787
The U.S. Constitution is written.

1788
April 28, Maryland ratifies the Constitution and becomes the seventh state.

1791
Maryland gives land to the United States for the capital of the country.

1800

1812–15
The United States and Great Britain fight the War of 1812.

1814
Maryland troops stop the British at Fort McHenry, inspiring the writing of "The Star-Spangled Banner."

1829
Chesapeake and Delaware Canal opens.

1830
The Indian Removal Act forces eastern Native American groups to relocate west of the Mississippi River.

1830
Baltimore & Ohio Railroad, first in the nation, opens for regularly scheduled service.

1845
U.S. Naval Academy is built at Annapolis.

1861–65
The American Civil War is fought between the Northern Union and the Southern Confederacy; it ends with the surrender of the Confederate army, led by General Robert E. Lee.

1861
Union troops take control of Baltimore and hold it throughout the Civil War.

1862
September 17, Battle of Antietam occurs, the bloodiest day of the war.

124

U.S. Events

1886

Apache leader Geronimo surrenders to the U.S. Army, ending the last major Native American rebellion against the expansion of the United States into the West.

1900

1917–18

The United States engages in World War I.

1929

The stock market crashes, plunging the United States more deeply into the Great Depression.

1941–45

The United States engages in World War II.

Camden Yards

2001

Terrorists hijack four U.S. aircraft and crash them into the World Trade Center in New York City, the Pentagon in Arlington, Virginia, and a Pennsylvania field, killing thousands.

2003

The United States and coalition forces invade Iraq.

Maryland Events

Baltimore fire

1904

February 7–8, the Great Baltimore Fire destroys 70 square blocks downtown.

1933

A hurricane separates Assateague Island from Ocean City.

1967

Race riots take place in Cambridge.

1983

Maryland and surrounding states agree to clean up Chesapeake Bay.

1992

Orioles Park at Camden Yards officially opens.

1995

Annapolis celebrates its 300-year anniversary as the capital of Maryland.

2000

2007

Maryland enacts the "living wage" law.

GLOSSARY

★ ★ ★

abolition the act of ending slavery through the passage of laws

biotechnology the manipulation of living organisms for developments in the areas of food production, waste disposal, mining, and medicine

boycott the organized refusal to use a service or buy a product, as a form of protest

confederation an association of groups that come together with common goals

conifer an evergreen tree that bears cones and needles instead of leaves

draft required enrollment in the military

estuaries mouths of rivers where the river's freshwater mixes with the salt water of the ocean, creating a variety of habitats

indentured servants people, often poor immigrants, who bound themselves to work for masters who paid the costs of the expensive journey to America and provided basic necessities; the servants worked for the masters until this debt was paid

indigenous native to a certain place

invertebrates animals without a backbone

locks devices on a waterway for raising or lowering a boat by changing the level of the water

longhouses long buildings made and used by Native American communities

palisade fence of logs set vertically into the ground close to each other to create a protected village

ratify to formally approve something such as a legal document

reefs ridges of rock or shell that rise near the top of the water, making habitats for other animals

secede to withdraw from a group or organization

segregation separation from others, according to race, class, ethnic group, religion, or other factors

tidewater low coastal land that is affected by tides

wigwams round, domed structures made of bent wooden poles and covered with bark and mats or hides, big enough for only one family

FAST FACTS

★ ★ ★

State Symbols

Statehood date	April 28, 1788, the 7th state
Origin of state name	For Queen Henrietta Maria, wife of Charles I of England
State capital	Annapolis
State nicknames	Old Line State and Free State
State motto	*"Fatti Maschii, Parole Femine"* ("Manly deeds, womanly words")
State bird	Baltimore oriole
State flower	Black-eyed Susan
State fish	Striped bass or rockfish
State dog	Chesapeake Bay retriever
State insect	Baltimore checkerspot butterfly
State song	"Maryland, My Maryland" (See page 128)
State tree	White oak
State fair	Timonium (late August–early September)

State seal

Geography

Total area; rank	12,407 square miles (32,134 sq km); 42nd
Land; rank	9,774 square miles (25,315 sq km); 42nd
Water; rank	2,633 square miles (6,819 sq km); 18th
Inland water; rank	680 square miles (1,761 sq km); 32nd
Coastal water; rank	1,843 square miles (4,773 sq km); 4th
Territorial water; rank	110 square miles (285 sq km); 20th
Geographic center	Prince Georges, 4.5 miles (7.2 km) north west of Davidsonville
Latitude	37° 53' N to 39° 43' N
Longitude	75° 4' W to 79° 33' W
Highest point	Hoye Crest, 3,360 feet (1,024 m)
Lowest point	Sea level at the Atlantic Ocean
Largest city	Baltimore
Longest River	Potomoc River, 383 miles (665 km), originating in West Virginia
Number of counties	23 plus Baltimore City

Population

Population; rank (2006 estimate):	5,615,727; 19th
Density (2006 estimate):	575 persons per square mile (222 per sq km)
Population distribution (2000 census):	86% urban, 14% rural
Race (2005 estimate):	White persons: 64.0%*
	Black persons: 29.3%*
	Asian persons: 4.8%*
	American Indian and Alaska Native persons: 0.3%*
	Native Hawaiian and Other Pacific Islander: 0.1%*
	Persons reporting two or more races: 1.5%
	Persons of Hispanic or Latino origin: 5.7%†
	White persons not Hispanic: 59.2%

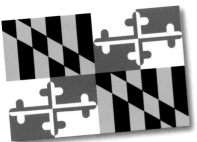

State flag

Includes persons reporting only one race.
†*Hispanics may be of any race, so they are also included in applicable race categories.*

Weather

Record high temperature	109°F (43°C) in Allegany County on July 3, 1898 and at Cumberland and Frederick on July 10, 1936
Record low temperature	−40°F (−40°C) at Oakland on January 13, 1912
Average January temperature	32°F (0°C)
Average July temperature	77°F (25°C)
Average yearly precipitation	41 inches (104 cm)

Coastal Maryland

Dominique Dawes (1976–) is a gymnast who competed in three Olympic Games. She earned one gold and two bronze medals. Born in Silver Spring, she has served as the president of the Women's Sports Foundation and supports many youth organizations.

Frederick Douglass See page 54.

F. Scott Fitzgerald (1896–1940) was a famed writer whose novel *The Great Gatsby* revealed the jazz age of the 1920s. He lived in Baltimore and is buried in Rockville.

Philip Glass (1937–) is a composer of operas, symphonies, film scores, and other works. He was born in Baltimore.

William and Mary Katherine Goddard See page 45.

Goldie Hawn

Billie Holiday

Dashiell Hammett (1894–1961) was a novelist who wrote detective stories and created the character Sam Spade in *The Maltese Falcon*, as well as Nick and Nora Charles, made famous in film. He was born in St. Mary's County.

John Hanson (1721–1783) was known as the "first president of the United States," because he was president of the Continental Congress. He was born in Charles County.

Frances Ellen Watkins Harper (1825–1911) was a writer and abolitionist. Born in Baltimore, she is believed to have written the first novel by an African American woman.

Goldie Hawn (1945–) is an Oscar-winning actress who grew up in Takoma Park.

Matthew Henson See page 61.

Billie Holiday (1915–1959) is sometimes called Lady Day. She was among the greatest jazz and blues singers of any era. She was born Eleanora Fagan in Baltimore.

Johns Hopkins (1795–1893) was an entrepreneur, abolitionist, and philanthropist who was born in Anne Arundel County. His fortune helped to establish Johns Hopkins University and other institutions that bear his name.

William Julius "Judy" Johnson (1900–1989) was a native of Snow Hill who became the first African American coach in Major League Baseball. He was admitted to the Baseball Hall of Fame in 1975.

Spike Jonze (1969–) is an actor, director, and producer who was born Adam Spiegel in Rockville and raised in Bethesda.

Munro Leaf (1905–1976) was the author of *The Story of Ferdinand* and many other children's books. He was born in Hamilton and lived in Garrett Park.

Barry Levinson (1942–) is a motion picture director born in Baltimore. His first major film, *Diner*, is set in Baltimore. Other films directed by Levinson include *Rain Man* and *Good Morning, Vietnam*.

Judy Johnson

Thurgood Marshall See page 67.

H. L. Mencken (1880–1956) was a journalist and social critic who was known as the Sage of Baltimore. He is regarded as one of the most influential American writers of the 20th century.

Kweisi Mfume (1948–) served as the president of the NAACP and was a Democratic congressman from Maryland. He was born Frizzell Gray in Baltimore, but changed his name in recognition of his African heritage.

Samuel Mudd (1833–1883) was the doctor who was prosecuted for setting the broken leg of John Wilkes Booth, President Lincoln's assassin. He was born in and practiced medicine in Charles County.

Isaac Myers See page 58.

Charles Willson Peale See page 82.

Nancy Pelosi See page 95.

Frank Perdue (1920–2005) was president of Perdue Farms, a chicken-producing company. He was born in Salisbury.

Kweisi Mfume

Cal Ripken Jr.

Edgar Allan Poe (1809–1849) considered himself a Baltimorean because that's where he began writing. It was there he created his famous poem "The Raven." Poe died in and is buried in Baltimore.

Emily Post (1872–1960) is considered the authority on etiquette. She was born in Baltimore.

Cal Ripken Jr. (1960–) was a shortstop and third baseman who spent 20 years with the Baltimore Orioles. Inducted into the Baseball Hall of Fame in 2007, Ripken was called "Iron Man" for playing 2,632 straight games. He was born in Havre de Grace.

Babe Ruth See page 85.

Pam Shriver (1962–) is a former professional tennis player and current sports commentator. She was born in Baltimore.

Robert Sargent Shriver (1915–) is a former journalist, politician, creator of the Peace Corps, brother-in-law of President John F. Kennedy, and father of television personality and California's first lady, Maria Shriver. He was born in Westminster.

Wallis Simpson (1895–1986) was the woman whose love for King Edward VIII caused him to give up the British throne. She was born in Pennsylvania but later lived in Baltimore.

Upton Sinclair (1878–1968) was a novelist born in Baltimore. His 1906 novel *The Jungle*, about the terrible conditions in the meatpacking industry, caused Congress to pass the Pure Food and Drug Act and Meat Inspection Act.

Jada Pinkett Smith (1971–) is an actress who was born in Baltimore. Her film credits include *The Nutty Professor, Madagascar*, and *Reign Over Me.*

Henrietta Szold (1860–1945) was an educator and Zionist leader who was born in Baltimore. She founded Hadassah, the Women's Zionist Organization of America.

Roger Brooke Taney (1777–1864) was a U.S. Supreme Court chief justice born in Calvert County. He led the Court in the *Scott v. Sandford* decision, which stated that black people were not U.S. citizens and thus were ineligible for rights under the Constitution.

Martha Carey Thomas (1857–1935) was a Quaker educator and feminist. Born in Baltimore, she persuaded Johns Hopkins University to admit women to the medical school and was the first woman to receive an honorary degree from that university.

Harriet Tubman See page 55.

Frank Zappa (1940–1993) was a rock guitarist, singer, and songwriter, as well as a producer of other people's music. He was born in Baltimore.

RESOURCES

BOOKS

Nonfiction

Allman, Melinda. *The Thirteen Colonies: Primary Sources*. San Diego: Lucent Books, 2002.

Burgan, Michael. *Colonial and Revolutionary Times: A Watts Guide*. Danbury, Conn.: Franklin Watts, 2003.

Jensen, Ann. *Leonard Cavert and the Maryland Adventure*. Centreville, Md.: Cornell Maritime Press, 1998.

Jensen, Ann. *The World Turned Upside Down: Children of 1776*. Centreville, Md.: Cornell Maritime Press, 2001.

Lake, Matt. *Weird Maryland*. New York: Sterling, 2006.

Leese, Jennifer. *Uniquely Maryland*. Chicago: Heinemann, 2003.

Lough, Loree. *Lord Baltimore: English Politician and Colonist*. Philadelphia: Chelsea House, 2000.

Stefoff, Rebecca. *Colonial Life*. Tarrytown, N.Y.: Benchmark Books, 2003.

Streissguth, Tom. *Maryland*. San Diego: Lucent Books, 2002.

Fiction

Carbone, Elisa. *Stealing Freedom*. New York: Knopf, 1998.

Hahn, Mary Downing. *Stepping on the Cracks*. New York: Clarion, 1991.

Paterson, Katherine. *The Great Gilly Hopkins*. New York: Crowell, 1978.

Paterson, Katherine. *Jacob Have I Loved*. New York: Crowell, 1980.

Rodowsky, Colby. *Hannah in Between*. New York: Farrar, Straus, & Giroux, 1994.

Warner, Gertrude Chandler. *Mystery of the Tiger's Eye*. Morton Grove, Ill.: Albert Whitman, 2001.

DVDs

Discoveries . . . America, Maryland. Bennett-Watt Entertainment, 2005.

Frederick Douglass. A&E Television Network, 1994.

Haunted Baltimore. A&E Home Video, 2006.

Our Century: U.S. Naval Academy: 150 Years in Annapolis. A&E Home Video, 1995.

Slave Catchers, Slave Resisters. A&E Home Video, 2005.

Underground Railroad. A&E Home Video, 2003.

Wild Ponies of Assateague Island. Coulbourne Studio West, 2005.

A Woman Called Moses. Xenon Studios, 1978.

WEB SITES AND ORGANIZATIONS

Chesapeake Bay Program

www.chesapeakebay.net/index_students.cfm
For student project ideas relating to the
Chesapeake Bay.

CivilWarTraveler.com

*http://civilwartraveler.com/
maryland/index.html*
For maps of Civil War action in Maryland.

Exploring Maryland's Roots

http://mdroots.thinkport.org/
A fun, animated, interactive Web site chock
full of educational videos, stories, interactive
maps, educational games, and more, all
aimed at providing children with a colorful
version of state history.

Maryland Digital Cultural Heritage Project

www.mdch.org
A digital library that provides readable, high-
resolution versions of texts, maps, posters,
and more that hold an important place in
Maryland's history.

Maryland Historical Society

www.mdhs.org
This Web site provides information
about current exhibitions, online exhibits,
brief histories, information about history
workshops, and much more.

Maryland Native Americans

www.sailor.lib.md.us/MD_topics/his/_nat.html
Links to Web sites for Maryland's indigenous
Native American peoples, all of which
provide students with cultural background,
genealogy, and contact information for these
different groups.

Maryland Office of Tourism

www.mdisfun.org
For a brief history and list of attractions for
every region and county in the state.

Maryland Online Encyclopedia

www.mdoe.org
Maryland Online Encyclopedia is an
enormous alphabetized online archive that
provides students with lengthy entries for
Maryland's important people, places, events,
organizations.

Maryland State Archives

www.msa.md.gov
The home for all government records of
permanent value dating back to 1634,
including newspapers, photographs, maps,
business records, judicial records, voting
results, and much more.

Maryland Women's Hall of Fame

*www.msa.md.gov/msa/educ/exhibits/
womenshall/html/whflist.html*
For brief biographies of every inductee.

Teaching American History in Maryland

http://teachingamericanhistorymd.net/
A reference tool for both students and
teachers, providing historical background for
Maryland's important events and landmarks.
It also features a series of online courses,
complete with syllabi, for kids to pursue on
their own.

INDEX

★ ★ ★

AUTHOR'S TIPS AND SOURCE NOTES

★   ★   ★

Welcome to Maryland! In writing this book, I've had a wealth of resources to call upon. I made a new trip through the state to remind myself of what I knew and to explore changes and spots I'd never seen before.

I made many visits to the library. *Maryland: A History of Its People* (The Johns Hopkins University Press) and *The Baltimore Book* by Linda Shopes were terrific sources, and *Maryland Trivia* was great fun.

Of course, I used the Internet, too. But I was sure to use Web sites that are from trusted organizations (such as those that end in .edu or .gov). The Archives of Maryland site (www.msa.md.gov) is particularly complete and fascinating. In the "All About Maryland" section, for example, you can explore the very complete historical chronology, take a tour of the Maryland State House, or see a picture of Margaret Brent. I found lots of information at the Maryland Historcial Society site (www.mdhs.org) and the Maryland Office of Tourism (www.mdisfun.org), as well.